AF287829

Lukas Stähli

Ingredients for a Fulfilling Life

Dedication •

For Lilie, our beloved Daughter
For Manuela, my beloved Partner
For Mum & Dad, my beloved Parents
For the whole Universe
Soul to Soul

Ingredients for a Fulfilling Life

Black & White Edition

Lukas Stähli

The German National Library lists this publication in the German National Bibliography; detailed bibliographic data is available online at dnb.dnb.de.

Typesetting: Herrn Meyers Buchmacherei, Cologne

Publisher: BoD · Books on Demand GmbH, Überseering 33, 22297 Hamburg, bod@bod.de
Print: Libri Plureos GmbH, Friedensallee 273, 22763 Hamburg
ISBN: 978-3-8192-6648-5

Contents

Prologue – the old Self

> It began in mystery, and it will end in mystery, but
> what a savage and beautiful country lies between.
> – *Diane Ackerman*

You and I can be grateful. We carry happiness in our hearts. We have woken up to the gift of aliveness. We can feel the day as we live it, recognizing each day's blessings and gifts.

Life is so dramatic from the very beginning. The abrupt cut at birth separated us from the secure bond we had with our mother. And despite, or precisely because of, all the challenges we face, the one life we were given is so precious. Rainer Maria Rilke's words, *being here is so much*, echo through me when I meditate on and contemplate my own life. Why is it, then, that we often become unconscious of our exceptional lives? Because we get caught up in the profundity of the ordinary. To be conscious of our extraordinariness, we must know what we really want to do, get disciplined, and act on it. This is why the act of writing about life itself feels like such a blessing. Significant questions and prompts invited me to ponder and search for answers in the depths of my awareness. Fully engaging with the written word gives the question more depth and meaning. Devoting my energy and attention to a question or topic opens up new perspectives and connects to other parts of life. Just to be quiet and meditate on the question triggers feelings and enables new thoughts that would otherwise be concealed in the infinity of my mind – to penetrate unconscious terrain, *terra incognita*, the conscious mind does not have access to…

The Quest for Meaning

As human Beings, we naturally desire to find greater meaning. We seek significance, purpose, and fulfillment in what we do and the paths we choose. Our Souls want to realize themselves. This exploration offers pathways to discover our personal insights into life's deepest inquiries.

If you're searching for reasons to get up each morning or asking **Soul-searching questions** like:

- »How can I find meaning and direction?«
- »How do I discover my mission in life?«
- »What is my life's calling – the mosaic of time?«
- »How do I connect my daily actions with my purpose?«
- »What steps can I take toward inner fulfillment?«
- »What would I tell my younger Self?«
- »What and who is worth suffering for?«
- »What do I think I am here for?«
- »What do I believe I need to do with my life? What is life going to ask of me?

...then this journey is for you.

Questions guide us

Why do we search for meaning? How do we find meaning? What gives life meaning? What is the meaning of life? And the meaning of meaning? Because we are questioning beings with a capacity for introspection. Is our quest to discover our authentic purpose? Why isn't simply going with the flow enough? Our capacity to reflect on our choices, values, and direction distinguishes us and drives this search.

To find genuine purpose, ask not just what you want but what you really want – discover the deeper motivation behind your desires. The **WHY**s behind the what and the why. For example:

- What do you want? – »I want to run a marathon.«
- Why? – »Because I want to prove I can do it.«
- Why? – »Because I receive accolades and want others to admire my perseverance.«
- Why? – »Because it gives me a sense of belonging and satisfies my need for recognition.«
- Why? – »...«, »...«, »∞.«

This line of questioning reveals whether the intention behind your purpose is to satisfy others, yourself, or both. Understanding your true motivation helps align your actions with your authentic values.

We humans are, by nature, in search of meaning. In a world that sells distraction, our hunger for meaning only grows – we are starving for meaning. We are that meaning-seeking, meaning-creating animal that tries to understand everything, wants to make sense of everything. Would not the greatest pain be the lack of meaning in life?

Sooner or later, we will think about life's meaning. Sooner or later, we all have an appointment with our Soul. None of us is going out of this experience without facing questions to explore life's depth. **Big questions trigger** us to seek **a more expansive view of life**:

- Who am I?
- What do I »know« from the beginning?
- What am I really looking for? – What do I really desire? – What are my deepest longings and dreams – my Soul's yearning?
- What has informed me and affirmed my right to be here, to feel what I feel, and to desire what I desire? And what gave me permission to seek what I want in this life?
- What matters most to me? What do I see as significant?
- What's the point of the life experience?
- From whence do I come, whither to, and in-between, what am I to do?
- Is this the life I desire, the story I want my future Self to tell?
- What does a day lived in personal happiness feel like? And in joy? In contentment?

What meaning means to you means everything! **You** are the source of meaning in your life. Meaning is personal and contextual. Every meaning is valid if aligned with your genuine intentions. This alignment creates integrity between your inner and outer worlds.

Focus on opportunities with gratitude and appreciation. See life not as happening to you but for you, as a teacher and friend. This perspective transforms challenges into opportunities for growth and inspiration. Remember, all disruptions are pregnant with new opportunities.

From Curiosity to Purpose

Doing what's authentic to us indicates what could be meaningful and fulfilling. The quest for meaning and purpose often leads back to our natural inclinations, talents, and passions. The path towards purpose typically follows this progression:

Curiosity (natural inclination) → **Interest** (focused attention) → **Habit and Hobby** (regular practice) → **Passion** (deep emotional investment) → **Purpose** (meaningful direction).

Curiosity, combined with an open heart, is the trigger for this journey to an integrated life. We are inherently curious Beings, designed to explore and discover. Children naturally start with what to do next rather than why – there's wisdom in this childlike approach of following what naturally draws us.

Finding our purpose requires both curiosity and introspection. Curiosity opens doors to new possibilities, while introspection helps us understand what resonates most deeply. Setting time aside for solitude allows our body awareness and intuition to reveal insights that daily noise drowns out.

Moving beyond dualistic Thinking

We tend to think in dichotomies – everything in pairs:

Good **or** bad / superiority **or** inferiority / left **or** right / black **or** white / day **or** night / peace **or** war / love **or** h… / light **or** darkness / sun **or** rain / north **or** south **or** west **or** east / North Pole (timeless) **or** South Pole (timeless) / philia **or** phobia / altruism **or** egoism / the Integrated Self **or** the Shadow Self / male **or** female / yin **or** yang / agonist **or** antagonist / centrifugal **or** centripetal / sympathetic **or** parasympathetic / withIN **or** without / past **or** future / here **or** there / YES **or** NO (maybe the most distinct and powerful words) / walk **or** talk / live **or** die (often do **or** die) / 0 **or** 1 / to do is to **be or** to be is to **do** / belonging **or** longing / success **or** failure / utility **or** futility / save **or** consume / abundance **or** scarcity / déjà-vu **or** 'vuja-de' / constructive **or** destructive / inductive **or** deductive / eustress **or** distress / salutogenesis **or** pathogenesis / cerebral **or** visceral / you **or** me / me **or** we (one letter turned upside down changes everything) / the observer **or** the observed / *la dolce vita* **or** overwork / utopia **or** dystopia / expressionism **or** impressionism / sense **or** nonsense / kairos **or** chronos / *Citius, Altius, Fortius* **or** *Lentius, Inferius, Debilius* / *Anima* **or** *Animus* / overt **or** covert / past life **or** future life? / universalism **or** individualism / individuation **or** conformity / attachment **or** loss / ONEness **or** multitude / finite **or** ∞ / …**or**…

The more extreme the opposites we construct, the more nuanced our understanding becomes – but only if we see both sides, both extremes. When the right and left eyes work in tandem, we are able to get a different picture. Contrast helps us find our way. As a counterpart to light, darkness creates space for reflection, intimacy, and the unconscious. When we only think and focus on one side, the other dissipates. Not to mention when we live only on the expected »good side,« when we suddenly overplease, or »over-love,« living in a high state, missing reality? – Of course, both lie on a continuum ∞. And how boring it would be to live only one-sided. Life is both, is all, anticipation and fear, nostalgia and disenchantment. A balancing act along the life curve.

We seek freedom and connection, solitude and the rich chaos of relationships. True peace isn't found in escaping life's complexities but in finding serenity within them. It's not just about living in perfect peace for the rest of your life, but experiencing peace in the midst of hardship. A sense of peace, a sense of freedom, a sense of…**is enough**.

In other words, there is no one without the other, the other without the one, but the ONE with the other. Don't make the cut, the split. When we accept both, when we embrace all, we are perfectly aligned.

In reality, we live in what poet Rilke called a »double realm,« in German *Doppelbereich* – not two separate realms, but one reality that simultaneously contains apparent opposites. When we dissolve rigid polarities, we recognize the full spectrum of existence. Everything is permanently impermanent. Maybe it's no coincidence that the words moment and **mo**vement share the same Latin root, *movere*, which means to move. Everything is in vibration, everything is in constant change.

We think we have to balance between the two states, the two extreme states, when, in fact, it's a continuum. One is part of the other one. When we see both sides simultaneously (which we sometimes see, especially when one word is part of the other, like FeMale), when we dissolve polarities, we are all and nothing, good and bad, big and small. Everything is impermanently permanent. Everything is colored by our point of view. It's always a matter of perception, perspective, a matter of projection.

When faced with decisions, we tend to limit ourselves to either-or thinking, assuming that there are only two options to choose from. However, in reality, at any point in time, there are infinite possibilities and paths to explore – the flood of choices. Life is an eternal spectrum, a continuum, a oneness, where every individual possesses a unique blend of traits and characteristics. Every aspect of life is interconnected, intraconnected indeed, and nothing works without its opposite. Therefore, we must recognize that we have every trait and aspect within us. Embracing our whole Selves can lead to a more fulfilling and meaningful existence. Instead of either-or thinking, we should shift our focus to **either-and**.

We are more than polarities. We are individuals in oneness. Deep Souls with bright Spirits. Our Souls cry for depth and multitude, our Spirits for universality and unity.

As humans, we tend to conceptualize everything, building mental frameworks to define our emotions and the universe itself. But the **uni**verse doesn't always conform to our categories. It moves holistically, leaning toward ONEness rather than dichotomy – a spectrum of all that is, all colors, all possibilities. This is hard for us to grasp, as we often think in binaries. Yet the universe operates with more nuance than our minds can comprehend. We are both light and shadow, containing multitudes. Only by embracing our luminous and darker aspects can we become whole – transcending beyond duality.

Thoughts on Life – Balancing Constants and Variables

Life contains both constants and variables. Like mathematics, certain principles remain unchanging across time (Pythagoras is still valid), while others, like theories in physics, evolve with new understanding. We must learn to navigate both stability and transformation, finding the right pace for our journey.

The ancient Greeks recognized two types of time: **Kairos** – the qualitative moment of opportunity, and **Chronos** – the quantitative measurement of minutes and hours. Understanding both helps us appreciate when to act with patience and how to value our days.

Life happens in the space between longing and belonging. It's an in-between state. From cradle to grave, we oscillate between breakout and homecoming. The impermanent dance. This tension creates the dynamic space where meaningful living occurs.

Finding Clarity amidst Paradox

How do we find clarity now in a world full of paradoxes? We are paradoxes, with emotions and feelings moving us in different directions. We humans are consistently inconsistent, trying to rationalize everything, to find the *ultima ratio*, even when our intuition speaks louder than rationality. An authentic journey will ask us to embrace contradictions, endure ambiguity, and resist the temptation to fall into either-or thinking.

Living with Meaning

A meaningful life looks different for each person. There is no single path or meaning, but there are meaningful ways to live that align with our deepest values. **Life is a canvas**; its meaning is yours to create by manifesting your inner vision.

You are the creator of the life you intend to live. Not necessarily an enlightened life, whatever that means, but hopefully an examined life, a more considered life, a life worth living on your terms. An expanded life that breathes meaning into the organ of meaning, **bringing your Soul to life**.

But is there a magic formula for a meaningful life? A syntax, a common pattern, a secret sauce, potpourri, tincture, or whitepaper for living the good life? A feng shui or geomancy? A higher order? What is **the secret of living a life worth living**? Is there a predefined **path to fulfillment**? Maybe… not. But there are tools from experience. It's helpful to gain inspiration, but crucial to integrate insights into daily living rather than keeping them as abstract concepts. This manuscript opens up stimuli, a toolbox to choose from, words or concepts, I call them **qualities**, to incorporate into your day-to-day. And it is my hope that it serves as a gentle spark of inspiration, like the quiet wonder a child feels when discovering the world for the first time.

Or shall we instead call it in search of a **mindful** or **wholehearted living**? Isn't wholeheartedness what brings meaning into our lives?

Contribution to others is a way of life, a lifelong commitment. In giving of ourselves, we often find purpose and meaning beyond what self-focus can provide. Our relationships become vehicles for both giving and receiving.

As Kierkegaard observed, *life can only be understood backwards but must be lived forwards.* This paradox reminds us that meaning often emerges in retrospect, yet we must make choices in the present with faith in their significance.

Choose yourself! – There is no duplicate in life, only one of you! Don't live in someone else's shoes. Don't try to replicate someone else's life, don't trade your genius and artistry for stability, but go **your own unique way**! This is such a miracle, hard to grasp! Mimicking others can inspire learning, but you and I must find our own paths. Your unique combination of gifts creates possibilities that only you can bring to life. You carry a distinctive energy, a vibrant life force within you (your very Being is a vibration) that will inspire others when translated through you into action.

Let your actions speak louder than your words. Meaning emerges not from what we say we value but from how we live those values in daily choices. Congruence between our stated values and our actions creates authentic living.

But what are the ingredients, the macronutrients for a (more) meaningful life? What makes life meaningful? Is it **significance, belonging, orientation**, and/or **congruency**? Or rather, deep **relationships**, a sense of **aliveness**, and **meaningful pursuits**? Another combination? I believe if we need one word to encompass it all, that word would be **LOVE**. The great heart of life that holds everything together. I ask you, is it not love that gives meaning to your life?

But after all, **what makes for a great life experience**? What qualifies to become a lifelong memory, a lifelong companion? What touches our heart, the archive of our intimate memories?

What makes a good day for you? – How happy you are? Or how happy you make others? Shifting the focus from self-centered to other-centered opens up new avenues.

Are you ready to embrace your Destiny?

Within each of us, there exists the quiet longing for a bigger picture, a desire for connection that transcends the trivial in our daily lives. When we cross the threshold of our comfort zone – often the oh-so-comforting misery of stuckness – and take decisive action, we move toward growth and meaning. This journey often lies beyond the familiar, the predictable, the safe, requiring courage to step into uncertainty, the uncharted path.

The path in front of you may be unclear and so intimidating. And this is OK. Otherwise, you are probably on someone else's path. Or in the words of Joseph Campbell, *if you can see your path laid out in front of you step by step, you know it's not your path.*

You have to really want something larger – really want it. When will you allow yourself to be what you want to be? What treasures of the heart want to be birthed into existence? – Off the beaten track.

The Essence of a Life worth Living

Inner contentment – peace of mind – forms the foundation of an integrated life. Without this internal harmony, external achievements often fail to satisfy our deeper needs for orientation and purpose.

Giving birth to your visions, dreams, and goals means bringing your inner aspirations – your larger picture – into tangible reality. This creative expression transforms abstract potential into concrete experience.

Life is a dance between awakening and surrender – between actively pursuing growth and accepting what lies beyond our control. This rhythm creates a dynamic balance that sustains our health on all levels.

We must try – even when it feels completely senseless. We have to try with all our young naiveté and sincerity, no matter what. This is part of the evolving process, especially during our younger years, the first half of our lives. Even when all odds are against us, we need practical experience to understand truly. This is part of the awakening.

You are **the ambassador of your own life**. How you live represents your unique expression of human potential, embodying the miracle of consciousness and choice.

Things don't just happen randomly – they happen justly. This perspective shifts coincidence to meaningful **synchronicity**, inviting us to look for purpose in what might otherwise seem chaotic.

Life is a question – truly a conundrum – and how we live our lives is the answer. Our daily choices, priorities, and actions reveal what we truly value, beyond what we might claim in words.

It's often not what you do that matters, but how you do it. How you make others and yourself feel – in service to the inside. This focus on quality of presence rather than achievement shifts success from external metrics to relational impact.

Don't die without being fully born. You are meant to fully awaken into your authentic Self and purpose – a rebirth into more conscious living.

Opening to the Essential

Open your eyes to what's essential. But what is essential? You decide! You know it, have always known it, felt it, though you may have suppressed it. Give it space and time to breathe. Feel it in your heart of hearts. The essentials are those elements that resonate most deeply with your authentic nature.

> And here is my secret, a very simple secret: It is only with the heart that one can see rightly; what is essential is invisible to the eye.
> – *Antoine de Saint-Exupéry*

The greatest adventure is the one within, the self-knowledge; knowing ourselves was the imperative in Ancient Greece. We are often strangers to ourselves. This journey inward can be more challenging and rewarding than any external mission.

There is never only one approach. Life is infinitely complex – that's its beauty. We all have different perspectives. How boring it would be otherwise! All approaches are meaningful when they carry a benevolent intention.

Life is a masterpiece woven from our experiences. We tell ourselves stories in this soap opera we call our life, good and bad, heroic and full of drama. We carry them with us throughout our lives. These personal stories have become our habits, our daily practice, our modus operandi – a self-fulfilling cycle. Or in Freud's words, »the repetition compulsion,« the inner drive to replicate the old, even if it's painful and leads us to stalemates. However good the story may be, there is always something. There is no »problem-free moment« in life, but we try to eliminate or solve the puzzle of overcoming our personal fears and lethargy. Every day is a struggle. Every day, our demons show up – a battle with ourselves to do what we are meant to do.

We are all fools to some extent and geniuses in other ways. The more we know, the more we realize how much we don't know – in fact, how little we know. Real knowing comes more from experiencing than studying. This humility about the limits of knowledge keeps us open to learning. This humility about our limitations and appreciation of our gifts creates the balance that protects us from arrogance and self-deprecation.

It's not what you look at that matters, it's what you see.
– *Henry David Thoreau*

Life's circular Nature

When we see time as circular rather than linear – like the Enso in Japanese Zen or the Celtic Circle – we perceive the eternal realm that transcends beginnings and endings. This perspective attunes us to life's natural rhythms and seasons.

We are constant wanderers and wonderers. Awe-inspired sojourners. Our minds and bodies long for exploration and wonder. This exploratory nature drives us toward new discoveries about ourselves and the world.

There is no wrong path – just teachers and stepping stones. Every journey offers learning, even those that don't lead where we initially intended. This perspective relieves the pressure of making perfect choices.

And we are already fulfilled. The rose blooms because she blooms – pure presence. No »why« is needed. And have we not already fulfilled ourselves at birth? The inherent completeness that exists beneath our searching. Life is a never-ending process, a constant death and re-birth.

Life happens in all its forms. We have to live through all cycles, joy and grief, calm and anger, altruistic and egoistic, to understand the deeper meaning – the meaning beneath the meaning.

The Space between Words

Silence isn't empty; it's full of answers. Sometimes, it speaks louder than words. In stillness often lies more wholeness than in speech. The space between words says more than the words themselves. Language cannot capture the fullness of experience.

With our words, we try to close the gap between experience and expression. But there's always a limit. Mathematically speaking, it's an approximation function. The better our choice of words, the better the approximation. The more the heart and Soul of the listener are engaged, the closer words come to conveying reality.

Questions without clear answers often lead to deeper understanding. Even when there is no answer (which is itself an answer), deep learning occurs. Sometimes, we cannot describe our knowing, but we know, deep down, what it's like. Life's mysteries will not be revealed by trying to find answers now, but by living our way into answers.

It's not about achieving some enlightened state but about accepting life in all its fullness with all its flaws and beauties. This is what gives form and depth to the human gestalt. It's a deep acceptance of what is, finding your way amidst infinite opportunities, embracing all emotions and feelings, gifts and challenges.

Let life question you. Live the big questions of life. Questions are the engine for our development and growth. Empowering the questioning process fires up imagination – maybe our highest faculty? – and raises energy. Some opening questions to explore life's depth:

- What has brought me to this place at this moment in my life?
- What does fulfillment mean to me?
- What quickens me – what fuels the Spirit in me? What touches me deeply – what feeds my Soul? Where do I encounter the numinous and luminous?
- Looking back over my life so far, have I experienced feelings of fulfillment? – How did I know I was fulfilled?
- What aspects of my current life are fulfilling?
- What is my task, my duty, towards fulfillment?
- When I review the words in the table of contents above, which resonate most with me?
- Why have I come to this book, or why has it come to me, now?

If you live them honestly, one day, you will live on the path to the answers.

Though Experiment

Imagine that you already have everything you want. You live the way you imagine it, the way you want it to be. You are already living out what you love to do. You live strictly according to your personal blueprint. Would you be more fulfilled then? Free from all worries? Would you have a more meaningful and beautiful life? Would you live the enlightened life – whatever this means? And if you only did what you love doing, what would it be like then? Do you think you would be more fulfilled?

Perhaps it is precisely the search for your own path in life that makes it so exciting – despite the hardships, the challenging moments, even the heartbreaking experiences. A path of sacrifice that leads us through the dark night of the Soul. Don't you think we would then long for such a life? A life we see now as negative, a life we wish to avoid. Do you really intend to cut the spectrum, the continuum, at a point where it no longer suits you? Wouldn't life, then, feel emptier, more boring, than if we embraced all the feelings – the beautiful, heart-warming ones, as well as the brutally tough ones?

We have infinite possibilities at any given time, but only one choice. In deciding on one thing, one way, we lose all other options. In other words, when we crave something, the one thing, we do it at the expense of losing everything else. This is the way life unfolds...The question, then, is: »Does this choice enlarge or diminish me?«

More Reflections on Life

Guess what? In life, everything is real – your imagination and your actions alike. The distinction between fiction and non-fiction, between autobiography and non-autobiography, exists only in the eye of the observer.

I believe meaningful pursuits are a strong driving force that gives us the energy to endure almost everything. Our Soul can handle a great deal of suffering. However, it cannot long tolerate suffering without meaning. As Carl Jung pointed out, the smallest of things with meaning is worth more than the greatest of things without.

There is no one-size-fits-all concept. When overused, curiosity can become noisiness; perseverance turns into obsessiveness. Even love becomes emotional promiscuity.

Yes, life sucks sometimes. It's hard just to keep your head above water, especially when everyone constantly speaks and writes about self-improvement. Don't miss playfulness amidst all the seriousness of goals, accomplishments, and achievements! Being curious and open to new things often helps. And to take yourself not too seriously.

Avoiding suffering can lead to a life that feels shallow and scattered – a life in numbness. And honestly, there is no life without suffering and sacrifice. Isn't it preferable to authentically and wholeheartedly suffer for something we love than to endure the unauthentic, slow death of doing something we don't truly desire? So, as we are going to suffer either way, I'm asking you: What matters enough to you that you are willing to suffer for? Do you sense the richness that lies within it?

Living life not reactively, meaning reflexively, but proactively, thoughtfully, and with nuance and differentiation, might be helpful advice. Our Soul is crying out to take responsibility for finding meaning. Or to paraphrase James Hollis, our Soul is waiting upon us to realize that we serve life when we step forward, take on that responsibility, and choose a path that truly makes sense to us.

Like a trailblazer or the thoughts of a thru-hiker:

Your heart knows the way. Run in that direction.
– *Rumi*

How do you deal with life? What is your modus operandi? I believe life is much more bearable if we let anticipation guide us through our daily grind.

My aim isn't to bring about a complete transformation or metanoia in your life, even if that's what you are looking for. Rather, I hope to offer sparks of inspiration that might ignite your curiosity. Think of these as seeds of possibility – ideas that might open new perspectives or questions where once there were only assumptions. When curiosity awakens, it rarely follows a straight path but often reveals unexpected insights. So, take what resonates, and let your wonder guide you forward. The most meaningful discoveries are those we make ourselves, driven by our innate curiosity about what lies just beyond what we know.

Now I invite you on the journey of a lifetime...

Life's Invitation

~

Life is an invitation, **accept** it
Life is a gift, **bless** it
Life is an opportunity, **take** it
Life is a mystery, **unfold** it
Life is a wonder, **imagine** it
Life is an adventure, **dare** it

Life is a challenge, **meet** it
Life is a duty, **perform** it
Life is a goal, **achieve** it
Life is a sacrifice, **offer** it
Life is a struggle, **face** it
Life is sorrow, **share** it
Life is a tragedy, **feel** it
Life is a test, **pass** it
Life is a promise, **deliver** it
Life is a puzzle, **solve** it
Life is a game, **play** it
Life is a wave/roller-coaster, **ride** it
Life is a song, **sing** it
Life is an echo, **reflect** it
Life is a dance, **express** it
Life is art, **create** it
Life is a canvas, **colour** it
Life is a treasure, **appreciate** it
Life is beauty, **praise** it
Life is a dream, **live** it
Life is a teacher, **listen** to it
Life is a mission, **fulfill** it
Life is a moment, **seize** it
Life is a journey, **complete** it
Life is a continuum, **experience** it
Life is a story, **write** it
Life is self-esteem, **value** it
Life is self-actualization, **realize** it
Life is a quest, **embark** on it
Life is a question, **answer** it
Life is longing, **satisfy** it
Life is belonging, **be part** of it
Life is love, **embrace** it
~

This is a plea from me to you: to live on your terms, to draw your own map, to share the brilliance within you – the valuable contribution that only you can bring to this world.

Life is a short pause between two great mysteries.
– *Carl Jung*

The human experience is bathed in mystery: Let's explore the short pause, the brief transit we call our life with 36 ingredients – nutritive qualities for the psyche, your Soul…

Lukas Stähli
Liebefeld, Bern

Part I: Foundations of a Meaningful Life

VISION — Seeing beyond the Present

ˈvɪʒ.ən

⠧ ⠊ ⠎ ⠊ ⠕ ⠝

[derived from the Latin *visio*, gen. *visionis*, meaning »sight,« »appearance,« »mental conception«; *visio*, from *videre*, which means »to see«]

> Vision without action is merely a dream.
> Action without vision just passes the time.
> Vision with action can change the world.
> – *Joel Arthur Barker*

Vision (to envision or visualize; visionary or visual) – the ability to see beyond the present – the profound mental faculty that distinguishes itself from dreaming. While dreams emerge from the unconscious realm, vision occurs in a fully awakened state of consciousness. Succinctly, a true vision is a spiritual revelation that unfolds while fully alert.

Between wakefulness and complete attention lies the state of trance vision, a liminal space where perception blurs and insight crystallizes. Vision is a transformative lens through which one glimpses potential futures. It is the gift of imaginative foresight – a mental landscape that reveals your unique God-given purpose.

Unlike competitive pursuits, personal vision is intimately yours, shaped by individual experiences and inner wisdom. It can be understood as a dynamic interplay of foresight informed by insight and grounded in hindsight, offering a preview of your potential path.

Your vision provides a visceral preview of what could be. To fully embrace it, you must allow it to breathe and expand. Pose a fundamental question to yourself: *What transcends my visual perception but resonates within my heart?* A genuine vision is vivid, living, and pulsing within your inner landscape. Immerse yourself in the feeling of your vision's fulfillment and observe the subtle paths your attention naturally follows.

The power of vision lies in its capacity to inspire imagination, spark creativity, and conceive unprecedented possibilities. To envision is to bridge your present Self with your emerging future Self – a profound act of personal alignment. In essence, vision is the transformative point where potential futures intersect with your current reality.

I personally thought that I had no vision or at least no clear vision. I didn't know what I wanted to be when I grew up. I only knew that I was good at certain things, like long-distance running or geography, but a vision? Over time, I became more and more aware of what I would like to do. However, it was more of a vague imagination than a clear picture, and that's totally ok. A vision can grow or appear suddenly. No stress, my friend!

Purpose, Vision, and Mission: Unraveling Life's guiding Forces

Purpose, vision, and mission are interconnected concepts that shape our journeys, each offering a unique perspective on our life's direction:

- **Purpose – The significant »Why«:** The fundamental reason something exists, something is created. This is your higher »calling,« derived from the Latin *vocatus* – a deep, often elusive concept that transcends immediate goals. In German, the complexity of purpose becomes apparent through its multiple interpretive layers, making it a particularly nuanced term to comprehend fully.
- **Vision – The guiding »What«:** It serves as a guiding principle illuminating the path to your purpose. Think of vision as a mental compass – a clear, inspiring image of what you aspire to achieve, to become. It provides direction and meaning, acting as a beacon that guides your actions and decisions.
- **Mission – The Practical »How«:** Mission answers the strategic question of HOW: It represents the concrete path or method to realize your purpose. In German, the term

Lebensaufgabe captures this beautifully – literally translated as the »task of life« – offering a more tangible approach to understanding one's life journey.

The intricate Relationship

Creative visualization emerges as a powerful mindfulness technique that harnesses imagination, mental imagery, and the power of thoughts. It leverages the law of attraction to transform abstract dreams into potential realities.

The boundaries between purpose and vision can be remarkably fluid. Sometimes, purpose and vision align so perfectly that terms like »destination« and »destiny« become interchangeable.

Life's Journey of Discovery:
- In our younger years, we typically focus on fulfilling our vision – a more immediate and accessible concept.
- As we mature, deeper, purpose-related, life-jolting questions begin to emerge, inviting more profound introspection and self-understanding.

This progression reflects the evolving nature of our personal growth – from the excitement of potential to the depth of meaningful existence.

Recognizing Vision – A Journey of Inner Discovery

Vision often emerges through intuition and inspiration and is sustained through intention. It begins with an inner sense of possibility, a spark of creativity that guides our thoughts toward the future.

Intuition helps us see what might be, even when the path is unclear. **Inspiration** fuels our desire to pursue these glimpses of potential. Intention, the deliberate commitment to act, transforms fleeting ideas into actionable steps, anchoring our vision in reality.

Recognizing a vision often requires moments of reflection

and clarity. These moments allow us to connect deeply with our inner intention, carefully aligning them with our values and purpose. It is a process of listening to the quiet yet persistent voice within, which speaks of possibilities beyond our current circumstances.

Why Vision is essential

We constantly imagine the future, sometimes merely to worry about it. As psychologist Martin Seligman astutely observes, humans are fundamentally *homo prospectus* – we thrive by continually considering our prospects. Yet, our ability to imagine the future often veers towards anxiety rather than inspiration.

We seek something to believe in, a higher aspiration, and an outcome to embrace. A clear and compelling vision serves several profound reasons:

- **Providing Direction** – Vision creates a path where none existed before. It establishes a goal beyond immediate reach but still within sight, transforming vague daydreams into tangible potential. By connecting us with our future Selves, vision illuminates the direction we truly want to travel.
- **Creating Clarity and Confidence** – A vivid vision is more than an abstract concept – it's a powerful mental blueprint. Carefully crafted, it provides clarity about our future and builds inner confidence. It enables us to focus on what matters most, helping us navigate challenges and grow beyond our perceived limitations.
- **Igniting Passion and Energy** – When coupled with deliberate action, vision becomes a catalyst for transformation. It triggers passion, enthusiasm, and drive, pulling us forward with an almost magnetic force. It inspires, energizes, and sometimes gives us the metaphorical wings to transcend our current circumstances.

Even when living within our personal bubble, a vision can be transformative. The key is to remain open-minded and curious. If your vision inspires you and you maintain a willingness to learn and grow, you are undoubtedly moving in the right direction.

A compelling vision is not only beneficial – it's essential. It can be the difference between merely existing and genuinely thriving, making it a crucial ingredient for a more meaningful, purposeful life.

Turning Vision into Reality – A five-step Process

A compelling vision should align with your purpose and values. Such a vision makes the journey to your destination more accessible. Being vision-driven fosters confidence and optimism, leading to greater risk-taking and growth. You don't necessarily need to be a visionary – someone with a strong image of the future – but you should at least set a clear and inspiring vision for your future. Only YOU know your imagination, so believe in it and never let anyone speak you out of it.

Several techniques and tools can help you formulate and ingrain a compelling vision. Let's be honest: turning what *could be* and *should be* into *what is* requires dedicated effort. Therefore, dedicate enough time and mental space to focus on drafting a compelling vision by asking yourself what you truly want.

Have faith in your vision. Craft it carefully, implement it with passion, and let the seed take root in your heart:

Step 1 – Imagine your Vision

Creating a vision begins with developing a deeply personal and emotionally resonant mental image of your future. Place yourself in a creative mental space where tomorrow takes shape in your mind. Visualize a future so compelling that it can guide your choices today and inspire your actions.

Your imagination is the invisible connection to your destiny. Focus intently on this future scenario, as a lack of attention – not imagination – often prevents us from developing a clear vision. Inspiration can come from various sources:

- Seek out an inspiring environment
- Find moments of silence and solitude
- Ask yourself reflective questions:
  - Who are you spending time with, and what are you discussing?
  - How are you spending your time?
  - What are you listening to and reading?

The most critical aspect is that the vision personally interests and motivates you.

It's also helpful to connect your vision to your current concerns. Resistance accompanies us on our way to fulfilling our vision. As Steven Pressfield describes it so well in his book, *Put your ass where your heart is*. Resistance appears necessary, but can be beaten with determination, integrity, and courage. In Thomas Edison's words, *many of life's failures are caused by people who did not realize how close they were to success when they gave up.*

Step 2 – Mapping out your Vision

To cast a compelling vision, ask yourself:

- Why is NOW the right time to act?
- What makes this season unique for me?
- Do I have regrets if I'm not acting now? and
- What is at stake?

Feel the vibrancy of your vision with every fiber of your body. Bring it to life by writing it down – preferably by hand. Trust your intuition and imagination.

When crafting your vision statement:

- Write in the present tense, as if it has already happened
- Use specific, detailed statements about your ideal future self
- Be concise and explicit
- Make it realistic yet challenging enough to be slightly intimidating
- Ensure it is inspiring and attractive, pulling you forward with momentum

Own & embrace your vision completely. Set your signature at the bottom of your statement to symbolize ownership. This becomes your north star and guiding principle.

Step 3 – Share your Vision

Once you have articulated your vision, share it with others. Be genuinely enthusiastic and committed. A vision becomes more powerful when made public, creating a sense of accountability and commitment.

Share it with your:
- Friends
- Community
- Wider networks

Transparency builds trust and helps you:
- Solidify your commitment
- Find like-minded supporters
- Attract potential collaborators
- Gain momentum

Step 4 – Sustain your Vision
Maintaining your vision requires consistent effort. The day-to-day grind can erode your initial passion, so develop strategies to keep your vision alive:
- **Repeat** your vision statement daily. The following manifestation techniques could be especially helpful:
  - Affirmations
  - Contemplations
  - Mantras
  - Meditations
- Write letters to your future self
- Record video and/or audio testimonials of your commitment
- **Celebrate** milestones systematically
- **Reflect** regularly on your miraculous new inner vision
- **Remember**: Inch by inch, your vision becomes achievable. Consistent attention transforms your inner vision into subconscious motivation.

Step 5 – Grow your Vision
Visions are not static. As you evolve, so should your vision:
- Be open to reimagining your vision script, to re-vision, and admit when adjustments are needed
- Share changes with friends and supporters
- Maintain commitment even if passion fluctuates

The fundamental truth remains: You rise to the level of your expectations. Your vision is a living document that reflects your growth, aspirations, and potential.

Ultimately, aligning your vision with your actions is your responsibility. Stay inspired, remain committed, and transform your vision from possibility to reality.

It's Your Move – Take Action

Every vision is unique, and life is full of challenges. Creating and pursuing a personal vision requires persistence and courage. While visions differ for each individual, transforming those visionary dreams into reality often takes longer than expected, and one encounters numerous obstacles along the way.

Stay committed to your vision, even when facing setbacks or resistance. This commitment means refusing to compromise on what matters most to you, even when circumstances seem unfavorable. Believe in your potential – those capabilities you have not yet fully explored – to achieve extraordinary things, even those never attempted before.

Begin by envisioning yourself at your most authentic: successful in your terms, fulfilled, and genuinely happy. Then, take deliberate actions that align precisely with this image. Adopt the mindset of someone who has already achieved their vision. When your inner conviction becomes stronger than external doubts or criticism, you know you're on the right path toward a meaningful life.

It's never too late to pursue your dreams. Allow your vision to guide you toward new opportunities and creative possibilities. **Act now** to breathe life into your vision, letting it energize and motivate you. May the clarity of your vision unleash limitless vitality – hold on and thrive! May the clarity of your vision unleash limitless vitality – hold on and thrive!

In a Nutshell

Vision is the ability to see the future and serves as a guiding principle that answers WHAT we aim to achieve. It distinguishes itself from purpose, the WHY, and mission, the HOW, by providing clarity and direction for our intentions. Vision emerges through intuition and inspiration, connecting us to our future Selves, encouraging confidence, and propelling us forward.

Vision is fulfilled through action, and action must be characterized by vision. Turning vision into reality requires imagining and scripting it, owning and sharing it, reinforcing it through repetition and reflection, and adapting, re-visioning it when necessary. A clear and compelling vision fosters resilience, focus, and momentum, helping us overcome challenges and achieve a meaningful life.

My friend, embrace your vision, take action, and let it lead you to fulfillment.

Reflective Questions

The following questions will help you find your compelling vision. The idea is **to imagine a tomorrow compelling enough to guide your choices today**.

1. What inspires you throughout the day?
2. What is your inner voice of prosperity whispering to you?
3. What do you think and ponder most of the time?
4. What keeps you alive during the night?
5. What activity do you love to practice?
6. Think you are standing in the future:
    a. What do you see yourself as in a couple of years?
    b. What do you see?
    c. What does it look like?

Wake-up Prompts

1. What's YOUR BEST? → When are you most energized, in full flow, contribute best? Try to bring yourself into this state so that you are able to excel. Now feel, believe, and let your hand and pen speak. Remember to keep it concise, clear, and inspiring.
2. Relax and draw your ideal environment and how you interact in it. You are the creator of your future! Imagine yourself living your vision. What do you see, hear, and feel? Sense the outcome, the picture you see, with your whole body.

3. Think action-oriented:
   a. What small step can I take today to move closer to my vision?
   b. Who can I share my vision with to gain support or feedback?
   c. What habits or routines can I adopt to stay aligned with my vision?
   d. What resources or skills do I need to realize my vision?
   e. How will I celebrate milestones along the way to achieving my vision?
4. Reflection-oriented:
   a. Does my current vision excite and inspire me? Why or why not?
   b. Has my vision changed over time? If so, how and why?
   c. What lessons have I learned from past attempts to achieve my vision?
   d. Is my vision realistic and achievable while still being challenging?
   e. How does my vision align with my purpose and mission?
5. Write a letter to your future self, describing your life after achieving your vision.

PURPOSE — Discovering your WHY
ˈpɜːr.pəs

[**a:** from Latin *proponere*, which means »to propose« or »to put forward«; **b:** over time, in Middle English, the word came to mean »an aim,« »intention,« or »reason for doing something«]

> The meaning of life is to find your gift.
> The purpose of life is to give it away.
> – *Pablo Picasso*

Purpose (to purpose, purposeful/purposive/purposeless) – **the overarching reason** – the big **WHY** – behind a person's actions. Sometimes referred to as life's »ultimate goal.« It serves as the driving force that propels us toward desired outcomes while helping us maintain focus and commitment. Purpose speaks to our intention and the direction we choose to orient our lives toward. Understanding our purpose can powerfully motivate both ourselves and others by providing direction and meaning to our efforts.

Personally, purpose is really where the path leads. This depth and vastness overwhelm me, exhaust me, and yet it sounds so rewarding. I rarely asked myself: What is the purpose of life, of my life? I mainly started by thinking about what I would most like to do. Often, purpose stands distant, too big to grasp, too massive to hold. It unfolds over time. It's more encountered than designed, at least for me.

Beyond Motivation
– The deeper Currents of Purpose & Meaning

Motivation differs from purpose in its nature and sustainability. While purpose represents a stable, enduring Why, the overarching Why, motivation tends to be short-term and mercurial, the more petite why. It fuels our daily actions in waves, often running out in the face of everyday challenges.

Our personal purpose(s) achieve their most significant impact when linked to a sense of meaning. They are interconnected but not the same:

- Purpose provides direction while meaning offers depth and reflection to our experiences

Together, they create a comprehensive framework that guides our choices, even when momentary motivation falters.

Historical Perspectives on Purpose

The concept of purpose has deep philosophical roots. In Greek tradition, it was connected to the *daimon* – a benevolent guiding Spirit that connects individuals to their Source and destiny. This concept suggests that awakening our inner Spirit links us to the larger energies, to our higher calling.

Aristotle later introduced the term *telos*, which became the foundation for teleology – the study of purposiveness and the examination of objects about their aims, intentions, and ultimate purposes.

One single Purpose, multiple Purposes, or a Sense of Purpose?

Rather than debating whether we have one defining purpose (as the one higher overarching Purpose) or many, it may be more practical to view purpose as a journey with incremental purposes along life's path - as meaningful pursuits. This perspective emphasizes fulfilling our existence as spiritual Beings (the infinite) with human bodies (the finite – the decaying matter) while maintaining good intentions.

By focusing on positive intentions – as defined by our moral compass – we cultivate beneficial actions in life. This requires mindful attention to our thoughts, feelings, and behaviors.

Another approach is to focus less on a single, definitive purpose and more on our feelings about purpose. We often experience a sense of purpose that guides us throughout our lives. We may feel that something greater is steering us, even if we cannot fully grasp it – more of an inspirational force than a concrete definition.

That's why I like to think of purpose as meaningful pursuits. We are on an endless journey guided by our hearts' yearning for meaning. If we act in a helpful way, filled with good intentions, we are on a purposeful path.

Finding your Purpose

When exploring our purpose, we can delve deeper by asking ourselves three progressively profound questions:

- Why does it matter?
- Why is that important to me?
- Why is that so deeply important to me?

We were created **on purpose, with a purpose**, and **for a purpose**. We were chosen to do the greater work. Therefore, every step we take is infused with meaning. But how can we truly know and find our purpose(s)?

Maybe you experienced a sky-opening moment – a defining instant that illuminated your path? If not, don't worry. It's completely normal to feel uncertain or lost at times. Finding purpose is a nuanced journey that requires time, self-reflection, patience, and openness to new experiences. Explore your interests, understand your core values, and identify what brings you genuine fulfillment. Trust that your path will gradually become clearer.

Finding purpose is a never-ending pursuit of becoming your ideal Self – a constant work in progress. In this profound sense, your purpose will be fully revealed at the threshold of the invisible life. Our physical earthly existence is but a step towards the ultimate transparency of the Self.

Practical Steps to discover your Purpose

Purpose isn't something that comes to you; it's something you discover within yourself. It has always been a part of you. Unlocking your purpose can be a challenging but immensely rewarding process. Here are a few tips that may help you along the way:

- **Reflect on your interests and passions**:
  - Examine what brings you joy and fulfillment
  - Consider the activities you enjoy in your free time
  - Identify topics or issues that truly excite you
- **Identify your values**:
  - Explore the principles you hold most dear
  - Envision the type of person you want to become
  - Reflect on the impact you wish to make in the world
- **Recognize your strengths**:
  - Assess your natural talents and skills
  - Consider how you can use these strengths to contribute meaningfully
- **Embrace new opportunities**:
  - Step beyond your comfort zone
  - Try new experiences
  - Remain open to unexpected discoveries

Finding your purpose is a journey, not a destination. It's a process that can unfold over years, decades, or even a lifetime. Your path may look like this:

Curiosity → Interest → Passion → Purpose

This progression reveals our incremental purposes along the way. Purpose often emerges when we apply our passions in service to others.

Curiosity is the catalyst for personal growth and purpose discovery. It's not about what you do but how you do it. Purpose is a daily practice, a choice we make to align our actions with our deepest values and passions.

Remember, it's okay if your purpose evolves. Embrace the journey, stay curious, and trust in your unfolding path.

Thought Experiment

Think of yourself as born and chosen for a reason – your unique purpose. Each day you're given is an opportunity to live out this purpose. Nothing exists without meaning. Everything happens for something or someone.

The very fact that you are here on this planet is a great gift – perhaps your greatest gift. No matter how dark your world may feel, you were given a reason to be here on Earth.

Someone is deeply thankful for your existence. Someone needs you, even if you don't fully realize it at this moment. You are a door opener for somebody, and this person is eternally grateful that you are here.

When I hear Purpose, I think of...

Destiny – I've dedicated my life to... – Lebensinhalt und Lebensaufgabe – Bestimmung – dedication – devotion – higher meaning – higher calling – higher task – my Soul knows the meaning and purpose of my life – having an appointment with my Soul – the journey of the Soul – telos – teleology – inner Spirit – YOUR purpose – higher aim – direction – the reason for being – the reason for getting up – precious gift – what is life asking for me – **why** – eternal – being of service for others – the people I lift up – what is my reason for tomorrow – reason reaps results – what am I meant to do here – the basic character of our Being – north star – essence

In a Nutshell

Think of purpose not as one big destination but as a journey that unfolds naturally over time. It usually begins with simple curiosity – those little things that catch our attention and make us want to learn more. These initial interests can grow into genuine passions. And when we find ways to use these passions to help others or make a positive impact, that often becomes our purpose.

Your purpose might evolve as you grow older, and that's all

part of the journey. There's no need to rush or stress about finding your one true calling. Sometimes, it takes years or decades to discover, and that's perfectly okay. The key is staying open and curious, paying attention to what energizes you and brings meaning to your life.

Remember: Everything happens for a reason - what's yours?

Reflective Questions

1. Do you think a life of purpose is the purpose of life?
2. Do you think purpose is developed, given by origin, or both?
3. Have you already found your purpose? If so, what is your purpose?
4. Do you think there is a specific purpose in life for every person?
5. Do you have one or several purposes?
6. What are you obsessed with? What keeps you up at night? What gets you up in the morning?
7. What truly matters in your life? What's worth doing? And what's worth doing badly?
8. Do you think your path is already shaped?
9. What do you think about most days in and days out?
10. What would you do for free?
11. What are you good at? Are you pursuing it?
12. How can you help someone? Who around us needs a hand?
13. What are you most curious about?
14. What are your strongest beliefs?
15. What do you think your life's legacy will be?
16. Do you think your current work is already fulfilling to you?
17. What are you committed to and striving for?
18. Why are you here? What are you meant to do?
19. Is my life serving a greater purpose? Am I here to help others or just myself?
20. Can I grow and give today?
21. Is meaning healthier than happiness? Is there a difference between the two?
22. How can I contribute value to the world?

Wake-up Prompts

1. Try to think about purpose. What comes to mind?
2. Write down what you think of purpose. If you already have a well-defined purpose or purposes, say it to someone you call your friend. Discuss your purpose with a friend or other human Being and why you think this is your purpose.
3. The big picture you must remember today is that you are working steadily towards…
4. Try one new activity this week that you've always been curious about.
5. Interview someone whose life or work inspires you.
6. Write about a time when you felt completely in your element. What made that experience special?
7. Describe your perfect day, from morning to night. What patterns do you notice?
8. List three ways you'd like to make a difference in others' lives, no matter how small.
9. Reflect on the following purpose-related statements:
    a. I don't like it (the work I must do), but I do it anyhow (because I see meaning in it)
    b. I like it and do it
    c. I love it so much and do it for free
10. What do you think of Nietzsche's famous quote: *He who has a why to live can bear almost any how.*

VALUES — Defining what matters most
'væl.juːz
ⁱ. ˙ ⁞ ⁝. ˙˙ ˸

[from the Latin term *valere*, which means »to be strong,« »be well,« »be of value,« »be worth,« or »to have power«]

Our value is the sum of our values. – *Joe Batten*

V alues (to value, valuable) are the fundamentals, the principles you want to stand for. They can be deciphered as fundamental beliefs that shape our behavior and serve as a moral compass. In other words, they are a set of ideas about how you want to live your life and the kind of person you want to be(-come). While we typically adopt values from family and culture, they represent deeper ethical motives, beliefs, and aspirations, ultimately guiding how we navigate life's choices.

Our commitments are rooted in our values. Even if we're unaware, these values are ingrained in our subconscious. They are the lived experiences woven into the fabric of our subconscious and now shape our choices and actions.

Value means something genuinely precious, something I've built up over the years – a personal philosophy learned through my interactions with the world around me. While living, I've gradually realized what truly matters in my life. My values have this beautiful way of bringing everything together. They connect all the scattered pieces of who I am in a wonderful way. I know what I want to stand up for. Clarity comes to light.

Values and Character Formation

Values guide not only what we want to achieve but who we aspire to become and how we choose to face life's challenges. Julie Smith describes them as reflecting the actions you take, the mindset you adopt towards them, and the underlying motivations that guide those actions. These principles become the foundation for personal convictions, profoundly influencing both our self-development and our impact on others.

Values serve as the building blocks of our character. When we consistently live according to our values, we project authentic self-confidence and create meaningful change in our environment. In other words, influence can be both intrinsic, strengthening our own convictions, and extrinsic, inspiring others through our actions. This creates a positive feedback loop – living our values reinforces our character, making staying true to our values easier.

Core Values as Life Anchors

While we may hold many values, identifying our essential principles provides crucial guidance, particularly during difficult times. These core values

- shape our attitude toward life and our approach to daily decisions
- guide us toward our long-term vision while keeping us grounded in our principles
- build the foundation of our character, shaping how we respond to challenges and opportunities
- direct our behavior patterns, creating consistency in our actions.

Values naturally evolve over time, making regular reflection essential. Engaging in thoughtful discussions with those who share similar principles helps deepen our understanding and commitment.

Living with Authenticity

The true measure of values lies not in knowing them but in living them - as the saying goes, *actions speak louder than words*. Regular reflection and discussion with like-minded individuals can help us maintain alignment with our values as they evolve over time.

This reflection process becomes particularly enriching when shared with elderly individuals, whose values have been refined through decades of experience and personal stories.

When we live engaged with our environment and activities that align with our innermost values and beliefs, we feel more content.

In a Nutshell

Values serve as our internal compass, influenced by both personal experience and cultural heritage. By identifying and actively embodying our core values, we strengthen our character, make more confident decisions, and positively influence our communities. Regular reflection ensures our values remain relevant and meaningful throughout our life journey. Now it's your turn: Set your standard and live the values you value most!

Reflective Questions

1. Remember, when you become bigger on the inside, you become bigger on the outside: What are your high-priority values? What are your five top values that guide your life? What are the top three of them? Why do you think they are your highest values? What is your inward definition of success?
2. What do you think are less important values for you? Why?
3. What are examples of behavior that support your values?
4. What is an example of a slippery behavior outside your values?
5. What's an example of where you have fully lived this value?
6. Who is someone who knows your values and supports your efforts to live according to them? What does support from this person look like?
7. What can you do as an act of self-compassion to support yourself in the hard work of living according to your values?
8. What are the early indicators or signs are you living outside your values?
9. Have your values changed during your lifetime? How have they changed?
10. Do you think your value will change for the near, middle, and long-term future?
11. What do you stand for? What is your core?

Wake-up Prompts

1. Write about a situation where adhering to your values had a positive impact on you or others.
2. Imagine you are mentoring someone younger. What core values would you advise them to cultivate and why?
3. Reflect on a historical or public figure whose values inspire you. What lessons can you learn from their life?
4. Describe a time when you faced a value conflict. How did you resolve it, and what did you learn?
5. Disappointments and pain are part of life. Ask yourself: *What do I value more than pain?*

To get more clarity on your core values, it's helpful to reflect and reevaluate regularly through a value check-in exercise. Choose the values that feel most important to you, mark or circle them. The following questions help to choose your values:

- What values do you want to embody?
- What qualities do you aspire to have in this aspect of your life?
- What do you want to achieve with your efforts?
- What attitudes or qualities do you want to cultivate in this area of your life?
- What contribution do you want to make?

List of Values

Accountability / Achievement / Activism / Adaptability / Adventure / Altruism / Ambition / Authenticity
Balance / Beauty / Being the best / Belonging
Career / Caring / Co-creation / Collaboration / Commitment / Community / Compassion / Competence / Confidence / Connection / Contentment / Contribution / Cooperation / Courage / Creativity / Curiosity
Dignity / Diversity
Efficiency / Environment / Equality / Ethics / Excellence
Fairness / Faith / Family / Financial stability / Forgiveness / Freedom / Friendship / Fun

Generosity / Giving back / Grace / Gratitude / Growth

Harmony / Health / Heritage / Home / Honesty / Hope / Humility / Humor

Inclusion / Independence / Initiative / Integrity / Intuition

Job security / Joy / Justice

Kindness / Knowledge

Leadership / Learning / Legacy / Leisure / Love / Loyalty

Making a difference

Nature

Openness / Optimism / Order

Parenting / Patience / Patriotism / Peace / Perseverance / Personal fulfillment / Power / Pride

Recognition / Reliability / Resourcefulness / Respect / Responsibility / Risk-taking

Security / Self-discipline / Self-respect / Serenity / Service / Simplicity / Spirituality / Sportsmanship / Success

Teamwork / Thrift / Time / Tradition / Travel / Trust / Truth

Understanding / Uniqueness / Usefulness

Vision / Vulnerability

Wealth / Well-being / Whole-heartedness / Wisdom

Zeal

ORIENTATION — Finding your Direction in Life

ˌɒr.i.ənˈteɪ.ʃən

⠲ ⠃⠆ ⠔ ⠈ ⠲ ⠲ ⠆ ⠈ ⠲ ⠆ ⠲

[**a:** from Latin *oriens* or *orient-*, meaning »rising« or »east,« referring to the direction of the sunrise; **b:** from Old French *orienter*, meaning »to place« or »align to the east«]

> Efforts and courage are not enough without purpose and direction.
> – *John F. Kennedy*

Orientation (orient or orientate, oriented or orientational) is your personal compass that aligns with your higher goals and deeply held values. It serves as a guiding light, pointing the way forward and revealing itself through growth, flourishing, and personal evolution. Those who live in harmony with their internal guidance system feel a profound connection to their life's true path.

I honestly don't think we lack dreams or miss our callings, but we often forget to pause and reflect and are not conscious enough of our direction, the way we choose. When we intentionally move toward our potential and embrace our possibilities, our purpose(s) gradually unfold, and prosperity naturally emerges.

Why Orientation matters

What matters most is not the magnitude or speed of change – change itself is inevitable. First and foremost, it's about the direction we consciously choose. To consistently follow the path that feels authentically right for us.

Having a sense of why you are moving in a particular direction brings a profound sense of direction and purpose. It helps you feel that your actions are meaningful and align with your true self. This alignment gives clarity and opens doors to a more satisfying life by ensuring that your efforts resonate deeply with your inner values.

Orientation is a powerful generator of momentum and inner energy. When your actions are aligned with your orientation, you experience moments of intuitive validation – those profound instances where you instinctively know you are on the right track. These moments do more than motivate; they strengthen your resolve and deepen your commitment to your chosen path.

Orientation gives me...

Direction – a reference line – reference points – a compass of the heart – perspective – a worthwhile path – a sense of proper direction – a clearer trajectory – clarity, especially when I feel uncertain or stressed – alignment with my values and purpose – momentum for my future actions – meaningfulness – confirmation of what's right for me – focus when I'm distracted – a sense of purpose when I question my next steps

Differentiating Orientation from Strategy

Strategy, etymologically derived from the Greek στρατηγία (strategia), is the art of planning, creating a roadmap with deliberate stepping stones toward a clear(-er) direction. It primarily focuses on measurable outcomes and actionable processes, often feeling career-oriented or task-driven. When I think of strategy, I envision structured processes and systematic execution.

In contrast, orientation is more of a guiding philosophy or approach – a more profound approach centered on purpose, values, and decision-making principles. It transcends simply ticking boxes or achieving immediate goals. Instead, orientation ensures that your actions align with your inner compass. It is inherently intuitive and enduring, typically feeling more ethical and value-driven. Where strategy outlines the how, orientation illuminates the why, providing the deeper meaning behind what you do.

Both concepts provide direction, but they operate differently:

- **Orientation**: Anchored in content, values, and purpose – your north star or internal compass. It represents the fundamental essence of your journey.

- **Strategy**: Grounded in process and planning – the concrete, actionable steps you take to progress. It is the map that guides your practical movement.

While strategy offers the means to move forward, orientation ensures you're heading in the right direction. When harmoniously integrated, they form a powerful partnership: strategy becomes the vehicle, and orientation the guiding light. Together, they transform purposeful intention into meaningful action.

Why combining Orientation with Strategy matters even more

You don't need to meticulously plan every aspect of your life – trying to control everything can actually be counterproductive and emotionally draining. But cultivating a clear sense of direction for your priorities – whether in career growth, relationships, or personal development – can profoundly transform how you approach life and make decisions.

People find purpose through different approaches. Some individuals draw strength from detailed long-term planning, creating comprehensive roadmaps that outline each step. Others thrive by remaining present, making intuitive choices as opportunities unfold. Both approaches are perfectly valid, like choosing between navigating with a detailed map or following your inner compass while traveling. The critical element is discovering the approach that resonates most authentically with your unique way and why of moving through the world.

By combining the overarching sense of orientation and direction with the actionable structure of strategy, you set yourself up for sustained growth and fulfillment. Orientation keeps you grounded in your purpose, while strategy helps you translate that purpose into tangible progress. Together, they ensure that you're not only moving forward but advancing in a direction that feels truly aligned with your truest Self.

In a Nutshell

Orientation is your inner compass – a profound guiding force rooted in personal values and deeper purpose. Strategy, by contrast, is the practical blueprint that charts specific, actionable steps toward your goals. While orientation ensures you're moving in a direction that feels authentically meaningful, strategy provides the concrete pathway to transform that purpose into tangible progress. Together, they form a powerful approach to living – one that balances introspective wisdom with purposeful action.

Reflective Questions

1. What gives you a sense of direction in your life right now?
2. When have you felt most aligned with your values and purpose?
3. How does orientation shape your daily choices and long-term goals?
4. How does your current strategy reflect your core values and orientation?
5. Are there areas where your orientation and strategy feel misaligned?
6. What adjustments could you make to ensure your actions move you in the right direction?
7. How do you prefer to plan – are you more comfortable with detailed plans or flexible approaches?
8. What's your personal definition of success, and what strategy could help you achieve it?
9. How do you determine when to rely more on intuition (orientation) versus structured planning (strategy)?
10. What role does orientation play in staying motivated and focused during challenging times?

Wake-up Prompts

1. Write a short statement describing your current orientation in life. How does it guide your decisions?
2. Think about a time when having a clear direction helped you succeed. What made that strategy effective?
3. Write down three areas of your life where you feel you need more strategic direction.
4. Consider a recent decision you made. How might it have been different with a clearer strategy?
5. Imagine explaining your life philosophy to someone you admire. What would you say?
6. Visualize your »north star.« What does it represent, and how does it inform your actions?
7. Break down a long-term goal into smaller steps. How can orientation ensure these steps are meaningful?
8. Identify one area of your life where your strategy could better reflect your orientation. What changes can you make?

INTENTION — Setting the Course for your Journey

ɪnˈtɛn.ʃən
⠔⠞⠑⠝⠈⠎⠡⠈⠝

[a thing intended; an aim or plan]

Our intention creates our reality.
– *Wayne Dyer*

Intention – also intentionality (to intent, intentionally) – the invisible force that shapes our daily choices and steers us toward our deepest dreams and purposes. It's what truly drives our actions; not just about what we do, but the *how* and *why* behind everything.

Intentions feel more tangible than visions or dreams, but less specific than actions. Once good intentions are established, they encourage positive, deliberate behaviors that evolve into habits and a commitment to sustain them.

Intention is **the seed of creation** – the purest expression of your heart's wisdom finding its way into conscious awareness. And this true intention will be fulfilled because all of your focus, consciously and unconsciously, is now working on the action. In this way, intention becomes the silent architect of our lived experience, quietly but persistently shaping our reality.

The Heart of Intention

Living intentionally, with the purity of intent, is about making conscious choices that align with your deepest values and aspirations. When you live with purpose, your daily intentions naturally flow from that wellspring of meaning. And here's the beautiful part: The more intentional you become in your daily actions, the more you sense your life is purposeful. Deep down, we all want to contribute and make a difference in this world.

Every action we take carries an intentionality behind it – it's like the universal law of karma. The responsiveness of the universe is at work. It responds to the choices we make. Our reactions and consequences spring from these intentions, the cause, the Source, creating an intricate web where everything is connected. Think of it like this: Life is like a garden where your intentions are the seeds. The more care and attention you put into planting those seeds, the more abundant your garden becomes.

This brings us to the realization that every well-intentioned choice we make, every action with good intentionality behind it, is meaningful. If we do what is – what feels – right for us, it is right for all. Actions reflect us. Finding the essence of everything we do can change our understanding of our purpose and, hence, the trajectory of our lives.

The Power of Transformation

Remember that fundamental law of physics – energy can neither be created nor destroyed, only transformed? The same principle applies to our intentions. Nothing in life is truly lost; it simply changes form. When you channel your energy intentionally, you create a powerful current that carries you toward your passions and dreams. True intention, combined with motivation and determination, becomes the fuel for reaching your goals and ultimately fulfilling your purpose.

Or, from the other angle, consider the wordplay in »**in-tension**.« It serves as a metaphor for aligning with our actual wants, being »under tension« with what we really desire, like a gravitational pull drawing us closer.

Finding Your Heart's Compass

But where does intention really come from? Not from forcing your will but instead from listening to your heart's deepest wishes. As spiritual teacher Tara Brach beautifully puts it, *every heart will get what it prays for most*. That's why connecting with your heart is crucial – it helps you understand your deeper »why« beneath the surface reasons.

Living intentionally also means honoring your priorities.

What do we most care about in our one wild and precious life? We all have things that matter most to us, and when we align our lives with these personal values, we're following our Soul's most genuine longings.

Signs of an intentional Life

We communicate our intentions daily. The deeper we go, the more we start living who we truly are. According to Tara Brach, a liberating, intentional life shows itself through three key signs:
- **Manifestation**: Recognizing and expressing your innate potential
- **Embodiment**: Feeling your intentions so deeply that they resonate through your entire being
- **Presence**: Keeping your aspirations rooted in the present moment, because today truly matters. It contains everything we have.

What are helpful Steps to become more intentional?

The following practices help and support us in formulating our deepest intentions from our awakened heart, setting the direction we intend to go, and becoming more intentional in life:
- **Attachment**: Connect deeply with your purpose, vision, dreams, and goals – let them guide your choices.
- **Mindfulness**: Practice mindfulness to stay present and aware of your intentions.
- **Embodiment**: Fully embody your aspirations, letting them fill every cell of your Being.
- **Internalization and Manifestation**: Actualize your innate potential.
- **Retention**: All resolutions are only as good as they are applied and become daily habits. So, turn your intentions into habits through daily practice.

Remember, when you shift from mere attention to genuine intention, something magical happens. Your authentic intentions will find their way to fulfillment. Self-realization. In the words of Mufti Menk, *When your heart is pure and your intentions sincere, the Almighty has a way of making sure that everything works out for you.*

Living with Intention feels like...

Full-body resonance – a sense of alignment – being energized and focused – a sense of clarity and purpose – connected to a deeper purpose – more grounded and centered – deep commitment and resolve – a sense of peace and »rightness« of direction – a strong sense of »why« – natural – in-flow – alignment of the heart and mind – being guided and supported – putting the mission statement into practice – the framework of getting unstuck – paying very careful attention to the state of the heart.

The Rewards of Living intentionally

Living with intention transforms your life in profound ways:
- It prompts you to identify what truly matters and take meaningful action
- It inspires you to make each day count
- It sparks creativity in pursuing your goals
- It unleashes your inner power and energizes your purpose-driven actions
- It adds depth to your life and helps you finish strong

So, take a deep breath, let go of tension, and embrace intention. Let your kindness blossom into action. Let your intentions shine through everything you do. After all, this one precious life is yours to live with purpose and meaning.

In a Nutshell

Intention is more than just what you do – it's about the how and why behind your actions. Living intentionally means making conscious, mindful choices that align with your purpose, vision, and goals. Like a heart's compass, intention guides your daily decisions and stems from your deepest values rather than mere willpower. Three key signs of intentional living are manifestation – expressing your potential, embodiment – feeling it physically, and presence – focusing on the current moment. When you live with intention, you transform energy into purposeful action, making each day more meaningful. Your benefits include clearer priorities, motivated action, increased creativity, and a more profound sense of purpose in life.

Remember, good intentions lead to meaningful actions. Be the player, not the ball – don't just accept life, but actively lead it!

Reflective Questions

1. What is it that you most care about?
2. Are you choosing to live with intentionality?
3. How will you show up today? Have you set an intention for this day, the week, the month, or the year? What deserves my full attention today?
4. What do you sincerely intend to do and achieve?
5. What is your most authentic intention, the real reason why you do what you do? And have you given yourself time to let the answer resonate within you?
6. What strengths do you not fully utilize?
7. Who are you? Who do you want to be?
8. How can you better align your actions with your values today?
9. Where do you feel resistance in your body when thinking about your goals?
10. How does it feel in your body when you are fully aligned with your intentions?
11. How can you physically embody your intentions more fully today?
12. Ask yourself: *What's the energy of that specific thought you have?* How does it feel? Is it trusting, beautiful, supportive, magnetic? Then, ask: *What's a thought that encapsulates the energy I want to emanate?*
13. Are you being driven by intention or dragged by goals?

Wake-up Prompts for Intention

1. Pay attention to your intentions. Do you live according to your loving intentions? If yes, stay in your energy field. If not, write down where and why you do not live according to them. Try to live a well-intentioned life again. Never forget, all creatures were created in the image and likeness of God and are, therefore, essentially good.

2. Complete this sentence: »At my core, I truly want...«

3. Journal about what »living intentionally« means to you personally.

4. Write about a moment when you felt completely aligned with your purpose.

5. Describe your perfect day where every action reflects your intentions.

6. What do I need to say »no« to to say »yes« to my intentions?

7. How did my actions today align with my intentions?

8. What did I learn about myself today?

9. How can I set better intentions for tomorrow?

10. How can I channel my energy more intentionally?

11. Write an intentional letter about how you want to treat and be treated.

Part II: The Inner Landscape

INTROSPECTION — The Journey inward
ˌɪn.trəˈspɛk.ʃən
⠔⠲⠞⠗�⠎⠏⠑⠅⠨⠹⠑⠝

[the examination or observation of one's own mental and emotional processes; to look within]

> Knowing yourself is the beginning of all wisdom.
> – *Aristotle*

Introspection (introspect, introspective) or self-reflection – the process of looking inward and examining one's thoughts and emotions to understand oneself better. We are the observer and the observed. It is a **self-exploration** journey to welcome all feelings and questions and be open to the gifts of life. Befriend and witness every emotion and thought in your interior experience. Become a whole picture of yourself. Every aspect of it is a portal to your inner wisdom. Whether you are looking back at your past (retro-spect), being present with current thoughts and feelings (intro-spect), or imagining your future (pro-spect) doesn't matter much. Drawing the correct conclusions and taking the proper steps are more relevant and allow you to understand yourself more deeply.

Introspection can be applied to the entire body and thus plays a vital role in body awareness. Emotions are the vibrant markers of our inner experience, creating powerful neural imprints that shape our memory and perception. I am, we are better able to remember situations that have triggered strong feelings in us. They can be seen as a continuum, with stronger emotions leaving footprints in our memory. This is why feelings play such an essential role in introspection. As inherently emotional Beings, we humans experience and express emotions, whether intentionally or unintentionally.

Benefits of Introspection

Introspection can be a powerful practice for personal growth and development, as it allows you to identify patterns, beliefs, and behaviors that may be holding you back or contributing to your success. By engaging in regular self-observation, you can gain greater self-awareness, develop a stronger sense of identity, and make positive changes in your life. Through self-reflection, you can bring your personal thoughts and feelings into the present moment and gain clarity on how you truly feel. Regular introspection opens the door and keeps you close to your life force. The more often you self-reflect on what is meaningful in your life, the more light you will find to navigate you. The more you reflect, the more you see something you haven't seen before. You are developing what is known as an inner witness.

Forms of Introspection – Pathways to Self-Understanding

Introspection can be done through various forms. Maybe you find clarity through writing in your journal, letting your thoughts flow onto paper. Perhaps you discover insights during your morning run, when your heart is pumping and your mind is clear. Or maybe you prefer sitting quietly, letting your thoughts settle. Some people even find their deepest revelations during therapy sessions, having those »aha« moments that change everything. It is crucial that you give yourself some distance to recognize, to reflect with fresh eyes, to remind yourself that all is well.

Remember, you're both the explorer and the landscape being explored. Every thought, every sensation that surfaces is a clue to better understanding yourself. It's like being a curious observer of your own inner universe, watching thoughts and emotions come and go like clouds in the sky or waves in the ocean.

In a Nutshell

Introspection is your personal journey of **self-discovery**. By taking time to explore your thoughts, feelings, and experiences, whether through quiet self-reflection, journaling, or even during physical activity, you gain deeper insights into who you are. This self-awareness becomes your inner compass, helping you navigate life's path with more clarity and understanding. The more you practice this gentle art of self-reflection, the better you become at recognizing what truly matters to you. And isn't that one of life's greatest adventures?

Reflective Questions

1. In which situations do you feel most alive and authentic?
2. Do you have a self-reflective practice in place?
3. What are your strongest feelings, and to what event do they relate?
4. What is it that your heart wants to tell your mind?
5. If you look at yourself with a loving gaze, what shifts?
6. What is the one thing you wish you had known earlier in life that would have made your life much more at ease?

Wake-up Prompts

1. As R. M. Rilke so aptly described, *The only journey is the one within*. What does this quote mean to you?
2. Take time and write down your strongest experiences. Why, in your opinion, are they your strongest experiences? How did you feel in those situations?
3. The next day, write down all the feelings that you encounter throughout the day. Therefore, take some time to reflect regularly on your emotions.
4. On another day, give yourself just ten seconds to describe your feelings.
5. Before bed, reflect on: *What brought me joy today, even if it was something small?* Think about what made those moments meaningful.

INTUITION — Listening to your inner Wisdom

ˌɪn.tʃuːˈɪʃ.ən

⠲⠿⠮⠇⠨⠿⠮⠆⠲⠿

[the ability to understand something instinctively, without the need for conscious reasoning]

> Intuition is the whisper of the Soul.
> – *Jiddu Krishnamurti*

I ntuition (intuitive, to intuit) – when life speaks from the inside out. Have you ever experienced a moment in which you just knew? A moment when the answer was just there, within a milli-second? As if an **inner voice** gave you the answer? An inner feeling? Or a moment when you were suddenly compelled to act, without even knowing why? Maybe you have encountered someone, and at first sight, you knew you would like (or not) this person.

Something in us seems never to change. Something inside us knows us better than we know ourselves. It holds on to us our whole life, **a constant**. It's this unbreakable me. It always stays with us. This something wants expression through us. The light we so desperately seek will never shine upon us until we first let it shine within us.

You most probably have experienced moments like those above. This was your intuition – your »**gut feeling**« – speaking to you, guiding you, sending you a signal or an impulse. With intu-ition inherent in every human Being, we were given a most pre-cious gift. Even if you can't remember a moment like above, rest assured, you do have an intuitive sense. You might simply not re-cognize the impulses, the plethora of voices, or the cues for what they are, or they get suppressed under the busy lives we create. But life always speaks to us, reminding us, »stay with me«. It whispers. It whispers until it screams. Until the star explodes. The star that lives in your galaxy, inside your body.

When I perceive the inner music, I often recognize multiple songs, multiple voices speaking, but I tend to remember only the two extremes. This is because we are skilled at creating concepts and thinking in dualities. One of these voices, which I call the ego voice, often tries to speak louder, overshadowing the Divine inner voice – the voice of the heart & Soul. Instead of solely focusing on amplifying the Divine voice, it's important to acknowledge the ego voice without judgment. It's also part of us. Imagine gently letting go of this part. By doing so, we create space for the Divine voice to emerge more clearly, allowing us to align more deeply with it over time.

Intuition is an ability every human Being is born with (and it might exist in animals and plants too, though this book will not explore this aspect). Intuition is especially sensitive at a younger age, but it evolves as we grow older and with any new experience.

Why is Intuition important?

Intuition is a crucial innate ability, an inherent part of us. Anything around us, any stimulus and experience we encounter, whether consciously or subconsciously, is deeply stored in our subconsciousness – the unconscious mechanism that runs our lives. The accumulation of experiences in our subconscious builds the foundation of our intuitive decisions and actions. When faced with a situation that requires a decision, our intuition will make use of all that's stored in our subconscious and will give us the answer within milliseconds. This leads to very accurate and fast responses, so our intuitive decisions are much more appropriate than our rational ones. This underpins the book by Christine Clavien. Rational decisions, while valuable, can be biased by the critic within us and might not consider all information. Our intuition, however, operates at such a fast speed and wouldn't let the inner critic take over. It simply outrules our Ratio. This is not to suggest that you shouldn't use your Ratio. There are surely many situations in which a pro/contra weighing is to be made. In fact, society and the way we were conditioned often tempt people to act, think, and decide rationally. For example, I must take this job because the salary is incomparably good, even though my gut is telling me that the work does not feel right. And often we find ourselves thinking: If only I had listened to my gut feeling, I would have known better from the very first moment. These are the moments when we overhear our intuition.

How can you improve your Intuition?

As mentioned above, you are an intuitive creature. You can improve your intuition by starting to mindfully observe slight cues that are coming from within. Be mindful when you have to make decisions when you meet people for the first time, especially when you are out in nature.

Since intuition accesses information from the subconscious, it is important that you allow your body to connect to your subconscious. This is done by slowing down your brain waves, which occurs when you enter a hypnotic state. Achieving this state can involve practices such as breathwork, meditation, or simply calming your mind and body.

Additionally, certain physical activities, like running or swimming, which follow rhythmic patterns, can slow brainwaves and create an environment conducive to intuitive insights. However, activities that demand high cognitive engagement, such as team sports like soccer, are less effective because your brain remains in a heightened state of alertness.

Your intuition is guiding you to what inspires you. It is crucial to trust it. Only what is trusted can be practiced and refined. Trust that you always have access to your inner truth, and begin allowing this remarkable ability to guide you. By doing so, you can unlock the full potential of your intuition and let it enrich your decisions, actions, and experiences.

What sparks Intuition, and how does Intuition feel?

The inner trusting voice – the small part deep inside your heart that already knows what to do – listen to the music within – the Devine Self – returning to the Source – eternal song – the inner witness, the one who controls and guides from within, *Antaryamin* – water zodiac signs – conscience (*Gewissen* in German) – mirror of the inner life – coming from the Soul – my internal and eternal Self – *Ātman* or true Self – hunch – nagging feeling – perceptions by means of the unconscious – the leading uplifting heart voice among other inner voices – the invincible voice – inner dialogue – gut feeling – sixth sense – inner, innate wisdom –

life's constant companion – the bridge between the conscious and subconscious.

In a Nutshell

Intuition is that inner sense we all have – the gut feeling or sudden knowing that guides us without explanation. We know it in our heart of hearts – not what we feel momentarily, but what we feel throughout our lives. It's deeply rooted in our subconscious and shaped by our life experiences. While society often emphasizes rational decision-making, intuition can provide quicker, clearer answers by bypassing self-doubt. To strengthen it, practice mindfulness, pay attention to subtle internal signals, and engage in calming or rhythmic activities like meditation or running. Trust your intuition – it's a natural gift that, when nurtured, can help you make decisions that truly align with the authentic You.

Reflective Questions

1. Do I recognize my intuitive abilities?
2. How do I recognize my intuition? By seeing, hearing, knowing, and feeling intuitive information?
3. Can I recall a specific moment when my intuition guided me? What happened, and how did I feel about the decision afterward?
4. Do I have regular dialogue with my inner voice? What is my intuition telling me?
5. What is your inner dialogue like?
6. Do I trust my intuition?
7. How can I integrate my intuitive gifts more into my life?
8. Have there been times when I ignored my intuition? What were the outcomes, and what did I learn from those experiences?
9. Do I think an inner voice is an internalized outer voice? Or do I think the internal voice was always there?

Wake-up Prompts

1. Over the next week, keep a journal of moments when you feel a strong gut instinct. Reflect on whether you acted on it and how it influenced the outcome.
2. Spend five minutes each day practicing mindfulness or meditation. Afterward, write down any intuitive thoughts or impressions that come to mind.
3. Some argue that *intuition is more reliable than logic in certain situations*. Do you agree or disagree? Why?
4. Do you believe intuition is a skill that can be strengthened, or is it entirely instinctual? If you feel comfortable, share your perspective.
5. Practice your relationship with your inner voice. When the little voice pops up, let it speak and try to feel it as deeply as possible.
6. What do you think about the following quote by C.H. Parkhurst: *All great discoveries are made by those whose intuitions run ahead of their thinking.*

BODY AWARENESS — The Wisdom of the physical Self

ˈbɒd.i əˈweə.nəs

⠃⠕⠙⠊ ⠁⠺⠑⠁⠝⠑⠎

[the perception of bodily states, processes, and actions that is presumed to originate from sensory proprioceptive and intero-ceptive afferents, and that an individual has the capacity to be aware of]

> Through the inner body,
> you are forever one with God.
> – *Eckhart Tolle*

B ody Awareness (to be body-aware) is genuinely feeling at home in your own skin. It's the ability to notice the sensa-tions, movements, and emotions flowing through your body, multilevel, both conscious and unconscious. Being present with everything that flows. It's not just about knowing where your body – your human estate – is in space; that's part of it, but it's so much more. A deep awareness of and connection to your phys-ical Self as an integrated whole, where mind, body, and Spirit are not separate but part of one continuous experience.

Our body is the gate to the sacred. Body awareness is under-standing the tightness in your shoulders after a long day, the flutter in your stomach before something exciting, or the warmth in your chest when you feel joy. It's learning to listen to your body's whis-pers before they become shouts, honoring what it's trying to tell you. To sense our movements, our movement process, deeply, be-cause nothing works without movement - what shapes the light-ness of our movement and the quality of our doing and being?

My great passion is running, which I have practiced compet-itively since childhood. Until recently, I didn't realize how we hu-mans started running. Which muscles do we unconsciously ac-tivate? Isn't it a leg? The supporting leg? Thanks to a podcast, I realized it's our center, our core. At first, the center of our body moves in the direction we want it to. When the center, the upper body, moves forward, the legs follow – completely counter-intuitive. The whole human system moves. Consciousness gives us clues.

Body awareness isn't just physical; it's emotional and even spiritual. As Brianna Wiest puts it, *We are consciousness incarnated in a human body.* It is the connection to the deeper, formless dimension within us. The relationship between mind, body, and Spirit. A way of tuning into yourself and finding harmony in the present moment – being fully alive, fully here, fully you. Through this inner presence, Eckhart Tolle suggests, we access an eternal unity with the divine or the universal consciousness he often equates with God.

The Language of Body Awareness

Body awareness speaks in a subtle, universal language – one of sensations, movements, and emotions. We are living antennas, communicating through tightness, ease, warmth, coolness, and tension, reminding us to pay attention to these signals. Unlike spoken words, this language requires us to listen inward, observing without judgment.

Breath, posture, and touch are key elements in this silent dialogue, each offering insight into how we feel and function. By learning to interpret these signals, we build a deeper connection with our bodies, aligning our physical and emotional well-being.

The Body as a sacred Geometry

Where else would the Soul feel at ease if not in, on, and around our bodies? Our body is a marvel of nature, a masterpiece of interconnected systems, uniting the heart, gut, and brain in constant **commun**ication. The heart beats with life and emotion, shaping how we connect to ourselves and others. The gut, often called the »second brain,« processes more than food – it senses, reacts, and intuitively guides us. The brain integrates it all, linking thought, emotion, and action.

Together, they form a symphony that grounds us in the physical world while connecting us to something greater – the Spirit.

This connection transcends the tangible, reminding us that the body is not just a vessel but a bridge between our inner essence and the universe. When we honor this unity, we live in harmony, embodying both presence and purpose.

Senses and Sensations: The Gateway to Awareness

Our senses are the tools through which we perceive and interact with the world. They provide the foundation for understanding our environment and ourselves. There are many senses. According to Michael J. Cohen, we could have as many as 54 senses or even more. Some of the more or less well-known senses are:

The Core Senses:
- Sight (Vision)
- Hearing (Audition)
- Smell (Olfaction)
- Taste (Gustation)
- Touch (Tactition) – I often wonder why we forget how deeply rooted this sense is for us humans. From the very beginning to the end of our physical life, it touches us deeply!

Additional Senses:
- Thermoception – Sensation of heat or cold
- Equilibrioception – Perception of balance
- Proprioception – Awareness of the body's position and movement
- Nociception – Perception of pain

Lesser-Known Senses:
- Sense of time
- Sense of electromagnetic fields
- Language and articulation sense
- Ethical, humility, or appreciation senses

By engaging fully with our senses – not just passively observing but actively applying them - we deepen our relationship with the body and the world. And our own body is our closest relationship in life.

Balance and Body Awareness as strong Pairs

Balance is both a sense and a daily act of mindfulness. From the intricate processes of homeostasis, which regulate our internal stability, to the flow states achieved during activities like running or dancing, balance reflects the harmony between body and mind. It is also the healthy interplay of tension and relaxation.

In moments of flow, we lose self-consciousness and become one with our environment. Physical activity, especially in nature, helps us access this state, fostering a sense of oneness and effortless balance.

Feet: Our Sacred Connection to the Earth

Our feet are sacred. They are the direct link between our bodies and the Earth. They ground us, providing stability and sensory feedback. Walking barefoot or wearing minimalist shoes has profound benefits, such as:

- Enhanced balance, proprioception, and body awareness.
- Improved foot mechanics and alignment, reducing strain on the hips, knees, and back.
- Strengthening of foot and leg muscles, supporting overall posture and mobility.

Prioritizing foot health – whether through barefoot walking, calisthenics, or proper footwear – lays the foundation for physical and emotional balance. Happy feet mean a happier, healthier you.

Walk as if you are kissing the Earth with your feet. – Thich Nhat Hanh

In a Nutshell

Body awareness is more than a skill – it is a way of living. Like musicians tune their instruments, we must tune our instruments - our voice, our whole body. By attuning to the body's sensations, emotions, and rhythms, you cultivate a deeper understanding of yourself and your connection to the world. It invites you to honor the body as a sacred vessel and embrace the full spectrum of life's experiences, finding harmony in the dance of tension and release, movement and stillness, body and Spirit.

Reflective Questions

1. Do you take regular time for body-awareness practices? What is your most common body awareness practice?
2. When was the last time you noticed a sensation in your body? What was it, and how did you respond to it?
3. Are there certain parts of your body you feel more connected to? Which ones feel distant or ignored?
4. Can you recall a moment when your heart, gut, and brain seemed to be in alignment? What did that feel like?
5. What activities make you feel completely in sync with your body and mind?
6. In what ways do you feel your body connects you to something greater than yourself?
7. How does being in nature influence your sense of physical and spiritual connection?
8. Have you experienced moments of *heightened awareness*, where our senses become more acute and our attention more focused and receptive than in ordinary consciousness?
9. Do you think something inside of you sees and asks you, independent of your will?

Wake-up Prompts for Body Awareness

1. Spend five minutes scanning your body from head to toe. Write about any sensations, tensions, and emotions you notice.
2. Take a barefoot walk and try to concentrate fully on your feet and what you feel.
3. Imagine your heart, gut, and brain could have a conversation. What would each part say about your current state?

4. Try to focus on one sense at a time. Feel it deeply in your heart. Can you describe it?

5. Reflect on a moment when you felt perfectly balanced – in body, mind, and Spirit. Describe that experience and what it taught you.

6. Choose one strong emotion you've recently felt. Reflect on where it showed up in your body and how you processed it.

7. Reflect on the idea of your body as a sacred vessel. How do you honor your body's role in connecting you to your inner Self and the world around you?

FEELINGS — Navigating your internal Weather

ˈfiː.lɪŋz

⠋⠊⠇⠔⠛⠎

[*pelə* – or *pālə*, meaning »to touch,« »feel,« or »strike lightly«]

> The heart has its reasons, which reason does not know.
> We feel it in a thousand things.
> – *Blaise Pascal*

Feelings (to feel, feeling) move us. They can touch our whole bodies in an instant, sending shivers down our spine, making our hearts race, or bringing tears to our eyes. We are all emotional Beings (or doings), largely hormone-driven, and, in this sense, more biological than logical – whether we like it or not. As Tony Robbins says, *the quality of our life is the quality of our emotions*. Our emotions shape our decisions, color our memories, and influence how we connect with others. From the flutter of excitement before a first date to the deep ache of loss, these sensations remind us of our fundamental nature as living, breathing creatures.

Emotions are a constant prevailing current, a wave of all emotions, flowing through every moment of our existence. But they come in cycles, like the rhythmic patterns of nature itself. Women may be more sensitive to this as they naturally follow a stronger monthly cycle than men. We flow with the seasonal cycles of days, years, and life itself – from the morning's fresh optimism to the evening's quiet reflection, from spring's renewal to winter's contemplation.

At this point, it seems important to make a brief differentiation between feelings and emotions. Feelings and emotions are words we often use interchangeably, but there are subtle nuances. Emotions are like ripples in a pond, starting as sensations in our bodies – raw, instinctive, and immediate. They are our brain and body's first response to the world around us. On the other hand, feelings are the stories we create about those emotions. They form when we reflect, interpret, and give meaning to what we're experiencing. In this way, feelings sit at a more conscious, meta-cognitive level, shaped by our thoughts and beliefs. Together, they are the quiet language that connects us to ourselves and to each other.

Think of emotions as signals – your body's way of saying, *pay attention, something is happening.* But feelings? Feelings are the way we decide to understand and live with those signals, our interpretations. Emotions are individual notes, and feelings are the melody we create from them. In the words of the sea, emotions are the ocean, feelings are the waves.

Think about your heartbeat for a second. It's been there since day one, even before. This constant rhythm keeps you going. Every beat is like a reminder: *You're alive. You're here. You're feeling.* Pretty incredible!

Joy and sorrow often appear as a pair. The same applies to happiness and misfortune. From one moment to another, we can go from an outburst of anger to an outburst of courage. They should be seen as lovers rather than opponents – touchpoints where life feels most vivid. Life always comes in a full spectrum, the rainbow of emotions, life's continuum. There is no cut, no shortcut, no happy highway in life, but the fullness of everything, in everything.

The Language of Emotions & Feelings

Emotions and feelings have their own silent language – one that doesn't speak in words but pulses through our bodies, whispered in the rhythm of our hearts, tensed muscles, flushed cheeks, and deep sighs. It's everywhere in our bodies, including our movements, living conditions, and lifestyle. In everything we do. Cognitively, we locate our emotions in our hearts. Emotions arrive uninvited, like sudden gusts of wind. Anger might burn hot in your chest, sadness might pool behind your eyes, and joy may bubble up, light and free, as though your whole body were made of air. These sensations are primal, universal, and instinctive – the body's way of telling us something important is happening.

But feelings are where we translate this language into meaning. They emerge when we notice the wind, pause, and ask, *what does this mean for me?* Two people can feel the same wave of sadness, yet one may interpret it as grief and loss while the other sees it as a call for change or growth. This makes the language of emotions and feelings both deeply personal and profoundly human – it's a dialogue between our inner world and the life we live outside of it.

To truly understand this language, we must learn to listen. Allow ourselves to feel what we feel. Not to fight, numb, hide from our emotions, but to sit with them as guests, letting their stories unfold. They don't speak in logic but in sensations, images, and memories. And when we give them space – whether through writing, speaking, or quiet reflection – they teach us things we didn't know we needed to hear.

I truly recognized the language of emotions when I stood before a dead body, my dad's body. The shell, the flesh, remained, but the emotions were gone. What once made him alive, the pulse, has vanished, leaving only the Soul and the memories to connect us. The lively feelings that once characterized him were no longer there. A deep silence and awe surrounded me, followed by a profound gratitude for his presence in my life, in our lives.

The Weight and Power of Our Emotions and Feelings

Our emotions and feelings are more than just fleeting states; they set the mood of life, deeply connected to how we perceive ourselves and the world. They can either weigh us down or lift us up, shaping our actions, decisions, and even our identities. Most likely, you remember those events in the past when your feelings were triggered at the deepest level. The more intensely you feel the bliss of life, the more intensely you will feel the sorrow. Your heart is vast enough to hold the ecstasy as much as the agony, the excitement as much as the boredom.

The strongest emotions – the ones that make your heart race or your chest feel heavy – often become the most powerful stories in your life. These emotions and feelings, if left unspoken, tend to linger. They may hide deep in our bodies and minds, where they can fester, quietly affecting our lives. A fear that becomes a belief.

A sadness that turns into a story of failure. When we give those feelings a voice – when we write them down, speak them aloud, or even name them – they begin to lose their grip on us.

There are many different types of emotions, yet some are more dominant than others. Most of the time, we are only aware of the strongest emotion at the moment. The current strongest feeling takes control. Emotions shape our internal landscape, which is why it's important to consciously decide which emotions you want to carry into your day. Cultivating positive emotions, such as peace, joy, or anticipation, can simplify many things. Daily practices, like priming yourself with thoughts such as *I want to feel...*, or using a mantra like *I color myself happy*, can work wonders and steer your energy in the right direction. They work as an anchoring practice, helping you to gravitate towards your desired feelings of the day. Conversely, our actions also influence our emotions. For example, even if you don't feel happy, forcing yourself to smile can trick your brain into releasing chemicals that make you feel better. Similarly, getting up and moving your body, like going for a walk or exercising, can naturally lift your mood and reduce stress.

Financial Investments – One of the best Teachers of human Behavior?

I learned a lot about emotions and feelings just from personal financial investments. It isn't just about numbers – it's about risk-taking and emotions. Behavioral finance reveals how fear, greed, and overconfidence drive our decisions more than logic. Market highs tempt us, downturns terrify us, and past mistakes haunt us. By studying these patterns, I learned to recognize my biases and develop emotional discipline. But it's hard, very hard. Especially when there is a high risk of addiction, it is important to set strong boundaries from the outset and to keep reminding yourself of them.

Emotional Fitness – Why Expression matters

You know what's amazing about our feelings? When we let them out – whether through words, tears, or even just a long sigh – it's like this weight lifts off our shoulders.

Imagine holding a heavy stone in your hand. The longer you hold it, the heavier it feels. But what happens when you put it down? You feel relief. It's like finally being able to breathe again. And in that space we create, that's where healing happens. That's where we grow.

This is precisely how emotions and feelings work. Writing or talking about them is like putting the stone down. It doesn't mean the feeling disappears completely, but it lightens the load. It allows us to let go of what no longer serves us or to nurture what empowers us.

Sometimes, naming a feeling gives it new life. Instead of keeping it buried, you can bring it into the light, water it with understanding, and watch it grow into something more meaningful – a source of strength, clarity, or creativity.

Connection to our emotional Center: The Heart

Take a moment to notice your heartbeat. It's the quiet rhythm that has been with you since the very beginning, even before you were consciously aware of it. Your heart is more than a physical organ; it's a bridge to your emotional youniverse. All emotions and feelings live here. It pulses life through your veins, connecting every part of you. The steady rhythm of your heart is a reminder that you are alive, present, and capable of feeling deeply.

When you tune in to your heartbeat, you're tuning in to yourself – your life, your story, your emotions, and your feelings. It's a gentle invitation to slow down, to listen, and to feel what's really t-here.

Sometimes, connection flows from external stimuli. A »Proustian moment« – when a scent or taste floods you with memories – enriches your world instantly. Profound experiences stay dormant in your heart until awakened by these triggering moments.

In a Nutshell

Everything passes. Don't hold on! Express it!! Remember, what you reject, suppress, or resist persists. When you express what you feel, when you let your body speak, you lighten your load and give yourself space to heal and grow. Your heart, always beating, connects you to life and your emotions, reminding you to be present. Feelings are layered and complex, mixing joy with sadness, fear with hope. Embracing this messy beauty is what makes you fully, wonderfully human.

Reflective Questions

1. Think of a recent strong emotion. Where did you feel it in your body first? Why has it come? What is it asking of me?
2. What emotion feels most like home to you? Where do you feel it? How does it resonate?
3. When was the last time you experienced conflicting emotions? How did that feel physically?
4. Which emotions do you tend to welcome, and which do you usually try to push away?
5. What's your earliest memory of feeling deeply understood by someone?
6. How do you typically respond to big emotions – do you express them right away or let them simmer?
7. What emotion has taught you the most about yourself?
8. When do you feel most connected to your authentic Self?
9. What old feeling are you ready to release?
10. What does emotional strength mean to you?
11. How has your relationship with your feelings changed over time?
12. In which moments are you emotionally deeply touched?
13. Are you aware of Synesthesia? When your brain routes sensory information through multiple unrelated senses, causing you to experience more than one sense simultaneously? In other words, when senses merge. For example, tasting words or linking colors to numbers.

14. Daily check-in questions:
    a. What's the strongest sensation in my body right now?
    b. Have I given myself permission to feel today?
    c. What's one emotion I've been carrying silently?
    d. Where am I holding tension in my body?
    e. What story am I telling myself about how I feel?
    f. What does my heart need in this moment?

Wake-up Prompts for Feelings

1. Journal Prompts:
    a. »When I sit quietly and listen to my heart, I notice...«
    b. »A moment when I felt truly alive was...«
    c. »If my current emotion had a color and texture, it would be...«
    d. »The physical sensation I'm most aware of right now is...«
    e. »A feeling I find hard to express is...«
    f. »Today, my body is telling me....«
2. Exploring Emotions and Feelings – Give yourself enough time to feel!
    a. **Name It**: What am I feeling right now? Can I name this emotion without judging it?
    b. **The Body Speaks**: Where do I feel this emotion in my body? What does it feel like – tight, heavy, light, warm, cold?
    c. **The Story Behind It**: What triggered this feeling? Is it tied to a moment, a thought, or a memory?
    d. **Layers of a Feeling**: What else might I be feeling beneath this emotion? For example, is anger masking sadness?
    e. **Dialoguing with Emotions**: What would it say to me if this feeling could speak? What might I say back?
3. Turn toward your sensitivity and let your sensations shine in all their facets: Think of your feelings as colors, flavors, tastes, and aftertaste. Do some rainbow painting and let your feelings come alive on a canvas, which represents the image of you as a human living canvas.

ALIVENESS — Awakening to full Presence
əˈlaɪv.nəs
⠈⠇⠀⠨⠇⠈⠧⠲⠝⠈⠎

[the condition of living or the state of being alive]

> Joy is an inherent inner aliveness.
> – *Richard Rohr*

A liveness (being alive, alive) – the essence of being alive. The magnitude of our Being. The life within life. The joy of existence - thank your ancestors - manifests in varied forms and intensities. Characterized by vigor, passion, and high or elevated energy, aliveness embodies a feeling of vibrancy and enthusiasm, the thrill of life. The spectrum of aliveness is broad – it encompasses enhanced joy, bliss, liveliness, vivaciousness, spiritedness, presence, and even a state of flow, when we are in the zone. The charged life. It feels like diving into life, stimuli vitalization, or revitalization. Imagine the refreshing feeling of standing on a mountaintop, diving into cold water, falling in love, or even sitting in perfect stillness and sensing the life force within you, fully awakened, an endorphin rush. In a more abstract sense, aliveness converges to the high and low points of our life curve. It arises when we step outside a predictable range, experiencing the extremes of life. And we humans need to surf the whole spectrum on the continuum of our emotions. We all need the **up-and-down swings** on our emotional curve. This means we are truly alive. The more extreme the curve, the more alive we feel, the more alive we are. The question is, what is your preferred curve? And yes, babies live the extreme curve. They have less emotional control, so they can change their moods in milliseconds.

> Life is not measured by the number of breaths we take,
> but by the moments that take our breath away.
> – *Maya Angelou*

Aliveness is marked by heightened awareness, a sense of adventure, and a deep connection to the present moment. Something that happens in the here and now. This state of being finds expression in moments of joyous celebration, radiant energy, and an **unmistakable zest for life** – what the French elegantly term *joie de vivre*.

Aliveness and passion are deeply interconnected, and both have the power to set momentum free. They both invigorate us. However, while passion is often focused on the specific activity you prefer and love, aliveness transcends particular actions and is more of an overarching feeling. It is the experience of living the day to its fullest.

But what are we truly seeking in our daily lives? What drives our ambitions, choices, and desires? Often, beneath all of life's goals and challenges, we are striving for a sense of aliveness. This is the feeling of being fully present and engaged, experiencing life deeply with every fiber of our Being. Yet, amid the routines and demands of daily life, this sense of aliveness can sometimes feel elusive. We find ourselves longing for it, consciously or unconsciously.

Embracing the Fullness of Life

I have always been amazed by the aliveness and positivity of my parents. My father, in particular, was a source of fascination for me. He spent much of his time outdoors, rarely fell ill, and seemed to embody a natural vitality. This led me to reflect on moments when I personally felt most alive – moments when my body, mind, and emotions were fully engaged.

Through these reflections, I identified some common experiences that ignite this profound sense of aliveness:

- **Physical Activity**: Imagine the way breath moves through lungs, blood pulses beneath skin, neurons fire in intricate patterns. Engaging in intense movement or exercise heightens awareness of our breath, heartbeat, and physical presence. Workouts or activities that push the body's limits evoke a vivid sense of being alive.
- **Immersion in Nature**: Spending time outdoors, especially in challenging weather or environments, deepens our connection to the natural world and enhances our sensory experiences. It's often a radical amazement. Everything is and

feels wonderful and beautiful. Or to paraphrase W.B. Yeats: The world is full of magical things, patiently waiting for our senses to sharpen.

- **Love and Connection**: Moments of deep love, intimacy, and connection with others are powerful sources of aliveness. These experiences remind us of our shared humanity and emotional depth.
- **Relaxation and Release**: Experiencing physical relaxation, such as through massage or the relief of pain, allows us to feel our bodies more acutely and appreciate the contrast between tension and ease.
- **Gratitude**: Profound gratitude for life's blessings or for someone's presence can bring about an overwhelming sense of vitality and emotional richness.
- **Pushing Limits**: Giving everything we have in a particular moment – whether through effort, creativity, or determination – creates a sense of fulfillment and purpose that feels deeply alive.
- **Powerful Emotions**: Feeling every moment of existence. Whether joy, awe, sorrow, or love, strong emotions remind us of the depth of the human experience and connect us to the essence of life.

Interestingly, moments of aliveness often emerge in contrast to life's fragility. Witnessing loss or experiencing personal setbacks can heighten our awareness of life's preciousness. These experiences can bring clarity, helping us cherish moments of vitality and renewal. In the breaking of old patterns or the facing of challenges, we often discover new energy and purpose.

Moments of aliveness delight my Soul. At times, I experience such profoundly moving moments that I feel I would rather die than miss them. They stir deep emotions, speaking directly to my heart, and I savor their memory long after they've passed. These moments open the heart space fully, leaving an imprint of pure connection and joy.

The emotional Dimension of Aliveness

Aliveness is a pulse, a spark that runs through your body, waking up every cell. Waking up your inner fire. Your senses come alive – your heart pounds, your breath deepens, and everything around you seems sharper. Colors are brighter, sounds clearer, and even the softest touch feels electric.

It's a state where your mind is completely absorbed, where time doesn't seem to matter. Spiritually, it's the deep connection to something bigger than yourself – a feeling of belonging to others, to nature, to the universe. Aliveness is that perfect mix of energy and stillness, excitement and peace, where you're **completely awake to the wonder of life**.

The emotional realm of aliveness is where life's richness truly unfolds. It's the joy that makes your heart soar, the passion that fuels your dreams, and even the sadness that carves depth into your Soul. To feel deeply, whether in moments of love, awe, or even pain, is to tap into the essence of aliveness. Embrace the full spectrum of your feelings, let them move through you, and allow them to connect you more deeply to yourself and the world around you.

The Path to Aliveness

How do we invite those vivid, life-affirming moments into our everyday lives? The answer lies in creating opportunities for aliveness – deliberately seeking out the experiences that stir our emotions, awaken our senses, and reconnect us with the raw, untamed wilderness of our bodies. Because aliveness often speaks wildly to us (from our first encounter with life), playfulness can be the spark that helps us (re)discover it.

As John O'Donohue wisely observed, o*ur bodies know they belong; it's our minds that make our lives so homeless.* To truly experience aliveness, we must release the tight grip of the mind, our control tower, and instead tune in to the wisdom of the body. By listening to our body's needs and following its cues, we unlock an innate connection to the vibrant energy of life.

Aliveness often requires more than passive waiting; it calls for deliberate action. It asks us to step into the unknown, to embrace curiosity, and to seek out adventures that stretch our boundaries and intimidate us a little. It is by pushing beyond the safety of our comfort zones that we discover growth, vibrancy, and the »sweet spot« of life where energy and excitement thrive.

At its core, aliveness is a gift of presence. Embodied presence – what might be called an earth-body connection – is essential. This connection grounds us in the moment, allowing us to fully engage with the world, with ourselves, and with others. It is in these moments of presence that we feel the richness of life coursing through us, a deep and undeniable reminder of what it means to be alive.

Yet, for this vibrancy to flourish, we must care for ourselves. Our physical and emotional well-being are the foundations of aliveness. We can only blossom, thrive, and give to others when our own tank is full. Holistic health – body and mind – is the fuel that sustains our ability to live fully and passionately.

The double Flow of Aliveness

Flow permeates everything when we are at our best. For me, this is where passion meets aliveness. As an exemplum, my body often enters a complete flow state when I'm running. When both my muscles and my thoughts align in this flow, ideas pour out of me effortlessly. It feels as though I could write a book or deliver a speech in no time. Everything in my body calibrates. The faster I run, the more I feel like I am in slow motion and the clearer the connections become. To me, this is the double flow of aliveness.

In a Nutshell

Embrace the wild rhythm of your life and spend your energy wildly. What steps will you take to ignite your aliveness? How will you reconnect with your body, explore the wilderness of your emotions, and cultivate moments of profound presence? By embracing this journey, by **putting life into your life**, you open the door to a life brimming with vitality, connection, and the extraordinary richness of being alive.

Reflective Questions

1. What lifts your heart? What makes your heart sing?
2. When was the last time you felt truly alive? You were dancing for joy? Describe the moment in detail.
3. What activities or experiences make you feel most connected to your sense of aliveness?
4. How do you define »being alive« beyond the biological sense?
5. What emotions or sensations remind you that you are alive?
6. Are there parts of your daily routine that feel disconnected from your sense of aliveness? How can you change them?
7. Is aliveness purely a physical phenomenon, or does it have a spiritual or emotional dimension?
8. Can you feel alive in solitude, or do you need connection with others to feel truly alive?
9. How does awareness of mortality influence your sense of aliveness?
10. Are there times when »feeling alive« is more important than being happy? Why or why not?
11. Can aliveness be cultivated, or is it something that happens naturally?

Wake-up Prompts for Aliveness

1. »One thing I can get excited about today is…«
2. Close your eyes and imagine your most vibrant, alive self. What are you doing? What do you feel?
3. Imagine you could infuse aliveness into an inanimate object. What would it be, and how would it change the world?
4. Picture a color, sound, or texture that represents aliveness to you. Why does it resonate?
5. Imagine a day in your life where you are fully alive every moment. What does it look like?
6. Visualize your »aliveness meter.« Where does it stand right now, and what could raise it?

7. Write a short story about someone rediscovering their sense of aliveness after a period of stagnation.

8. Create a poem exploring the contrast between »existing« and »truly living.«

9. Describe a world where aliveness can be measured. What would society look like?

10. Write about a moment when you felt most vibrant and connected to life.

11. Write a piece that describes aliveness through the five senses.

12. Write a letter to your future self, explaining what »living fully« means to you right now.

13. Craft a narrative about breaking free from autopilot and embracing full presence.

14. Explore how confronting personal truths can reignite one's sense of aliveness.

Part III: Growing through Connection

RELATIONSHIPS — The Mirrors of our Soul

rɪˈleɪʃənʃɪps

⠗⠑⠇⠑⠊⠳⠷⠩⠽⠏⠎

[**a:** the way in which two or more people or things are connected, or the state of being connected; **b:** the way in which two or more people or groups regard and behave towards each other]

> There is no more lovely, friendly, and charming relationship, communion, or company
> than a good marriage.
> – *Martin Luther*

Relationships (to relate, relational) express the connection and intimacy between everything – people, animals, plants, planets, feelings, the sky. We cannot avoid relating to others, whether we like it or not. We are connected from the very beginning of our lives and crave, sometimes cry, to belong. Imagine our deep connection with our mother. In the womb, we were wired in communion, one with our caregiving mother and maybe sister(s) and brother(s). We were soaked in love. We know how crucial touch is from the beginning of our lives. Our safe bond with our mother kept us together until the abrupt cut during our birth; This is when we all experience for the first time how dramatic life itself is.

The understanding of intimacy differs in every relationship. In general, interpersonal relationships refer to the connection, interaction, and bond between individuals. There are several types of relationships, including:

- Family relationships
- Friendships
- Acquaintances
- Romantic relationships
- Sexual relationships

- Work relationships
- Situational relationships
- You name it...

These relationships vary significantly in terms of closeness, reliability, and depth. They also differ in how strongly they are self-selected (e.g., romantic and sexual relationships) or arise purely by chance (e.g., family and work relationships).

For me, to relate to each other is the ability to get along with others and the world. According to Robert Waldinger, warm relationships are crucial for our well-being. Being kind to each other brings light. We want to be reflected, feel seen, and understood by others. *Please make me feel important* is the fundamental human cry for which we give everything.

Why are Relationships important?

Nothing can be done alone. We got everything with the help of others. The fact that you live here, on this blue planet, now, is unimaginable and yet no coincidence. You were loved into existence.

Alone, I feel so naked; together, I am so strong. We are dependent on others, on the outer world. Relationships are integral to our lives and significantly impact our emotional and mental well-being. They provide support, love, and a sense of belonging. Strong relationships can help us navigate challenges and lead a more fulfilling life. They are essential for personal growth and development.

Good social relationships are universally important for the human mood and psyche. Studies show that people with close bonds are among the happiest (Seligman & Diener, 2002). Additionally, *social relationships improve lifespans: People in healthy long-term relationships are 50% less likely to die prematurely than people without them. In terms of life expectancy, living without these relationships is as unhealthy as smoking* (Holt-Lunstad, J., Smith, T.B., & Layton, J.B., 2010).

Thus, social fitness - fostering healthy relationships - is worthwhile for personal happiness and longevity.

We are not independent but intraconnected

Independence is impossible for us humans. It's an idea, but not more. We are all karmically connected Souls, deeply interdependent. We really are Soul friends, Anam Caras. I love the term **intraconnected** coined by Daniel J. Siegel, because it encompasses all connections, even »internal« relationships, the ones within. Everything is deeply connected and influences each other. Every part contains the whole. We are co-creators forever; we can not separate ourselves, never. We are time and space-dependent. I believe we are a union of hearts that endure beyond our physical deaths, growing toward one universal Soul.

How to keep a Relationship healthy

Once established, a relationship doesn't automatically last. To sustain a relationship, the individuals involved need to actively nurture the connection. This requires time, effort, and commitment. A healthy relationship can be maintained through various actions, including:

- Being supportive and encouraging
- Being trustworthy
- Showing interest in each other
- Showing appreciation and gratitude
- Communicating openly and honestly
- Being affectionate and showing that you care
- Demonstrating mutual respect
- Actively listening. God gave us one mouth and two ears!
- Feeling empathy for each other
- Spending quality time together
- Establishing and maintaining healthy boundaries

These actions should focus more on completing each other than competing against each other. By practicing these behaviors, we can foster strong, enduring relationships that contribute to our overall well-being.

The Relationship with oneself

In the whirlwind of our daily lives, we often lose touch with ourselves. Despite being »perpetually connected,« a deeper loneliness settles in as genuine presence becomes increasingly rare. This disconnection from our authentic Selves, our core values, and what truly matters to us is the real source of our isolation. When we pause and learn to listen inward again, tuning into the quiet wisdom of our heart and Soul, the Divine Light that dwells within, we can rediscover that sense of true connectedness and nurture it back to life.

In a Nutshell

Relationships are a vital part of our lives, shaping how we connect and bond with others, whether family, friends, or romantic partners. They provide support, love, and a sense of belonging, which are key to our happiness and well-being. Healthy relationships don't just happen; they take effort, like being trustworthy, showing appreciation, and spending quality time together. Investing in these connections can make your life richer, happier, and even longer.

Remember: **What connects us unites us!**

Reflective Questions

1. What key factors are you looking for in a relationship?
2. What does a relationship mean to you?
3. What are your musts and don'ts in a relationship?
4. With whom do you have a relationship? What type of relationship is it?
5. With whom or what do you feel you have the deepest relationship(s)?
6. What are your strategies to keep your relationships healthy?
7. What is born out of your relationships?
8. What would your future together look like?

9. What's the energy you create together?
10. How do you wish to co-create the future with your loving beings?
11. What is birthed out of your relationships?
12. How do you see intergenerational relationships
13. Do you believe in an *Anima Mundi*, a »World Soul«?

Wake-up Prompts

1. Reflect on a relationship in your life that has significantly impacted your well-being. What made it meaningful?
2. Imagine your future relationships. What should they look like? What are your wishes for your deeper relationships? Write down or draw how you imagine them to be.
3. What do you think of a collaborative and supportive tribe? An inclusive circle of friends?
4. Something that could have helped you feel more connected to others today would have been…
5. *I come as one, but I stand as ten thousand.* - Maya Angelou. Do you feel the force of your ancestors? Remember, you are never alone!
6. Try *Mudita*, the dharmic concept of joy, particularly the pleasure that comes from delighting in other people's well-being.

BELONGING — Finding your Place in the World

bɪˈlɒŋɪŋ
⠲⠐⠇⠲⠝⠰⠡⠔⠲⠡

[to be fitting, be suitable]

> If we have no peace, it is because
> we have forgotten that
> we belong to each other.
> – *Mother Teresa*

Belonging (to belong, belonging) is something we all long for. That deep, undeniable need to feel connected, to be a part of something bigger, to be loved. We all want to be seen, heard, felt, and touched. To feel understood, accepted, valued, and loved. Our Soul longs to find an outer mirror. It is intrinsic to the human experience. Love, in its purest form, is the ultimate expression of belonging. As a species, we are hardwired to seek connection, recognition, and the feeling of contributing to something greater than ourselves. This longing begins early, even in the womb, where we experience our first nine months in bonding, in benevolent oneness with our mother – a profound state of togetherness. We were looked after, cared for, and loved. How are we ever meant to truly separate from this foundational experience of connection?

Life happens in between longing and belonging. We long to belong. This is especially the case if you are a nomad. The Irish poet John O'Donohue believed that longing to belong is one of the deepest and most fundamental human desires. In his own touching words: *The hunger to belong is at the heart of our nature.* And he continues: *When you belong, it is as if you have come home to yourself, to a place of warmth, embrace, and integration.*

We all cry for recognition and belonging, clamoring to be part of a greater whole. This cry is not just about being loved; it's also about making a meaningful contribution and feeling valued within our communities and relationships. The absence of attention and recognition can feel like the absence of love itself. To be unseen, unheard, or ignored is one of the deepest pains a person can endure.

Elements of Belonging

Some key characteristics of true belonging are:
- **Authenticity**: True belonging happens when you can show up as your genuine Self without fear of judgment or rejection. It's not about conforming to fit in; it's about being embraced for your individuality. Or as author Brené Brown puts it, *true belonging doesn't require you to change who you are; it requires you to be who you are.*
- **Acceptance**: A sense of belonging comes from knowing you are accepted by others and that your presence matters. It involves feeling seen, heard, and understood. This does not mean agreeing with everyone on everything, but also enjoying your disagreements with them.
- **Connection**: Belonging often arises through meaningful relationships, where mutual respect, empathy, and shared experiences foster connection. In fact, what I have learned is that the most incredible experiences are the ones that are shared. This connection can be with people, communities, or even places that deeply resonate with your identity.
- **Contribution**: Feeling like you play an essential role within a group or space can strengthen belonging. When your presence and actions contribute to a shared purpose, you often feel more integrated.
- **Reciprocity**: Belonging is often mutual – the group or environment values you, and you value being part of it. It involves giving and receiving trust, care, and respect. When people feel you care about them, they listen to you.
- **Alignment with Values**: A true sense of belonging often comes from being part of a group or place that aligns with your core beliefs, values, or identity.

How does it feel when you walk yourself home to yourself?

Longing for Belonging – The human Hunger for Belonging

As human Beings, we desire stability and comfort, and yet long for growth and change. This fundamental tension shapes our journey. John O'Donohue beautifully captures the essence of our striving. *Our bodies know that they belong; it's our minds that make us so homeless.* Longing is a very strong driving force. We are inherently restless, always seeking growth, adventure, and new opportunities. This unceasing restlessness runs through everything we do. We're always searching. Whether through curiosity, the pursuit of aliveness, or even the need to prove something to ourselves or others. Our thoughts often wander to new goals – what's next, where we're going, or even what we'll eat. Yet, beneath these pursuits lies a **deeper cry: the longing to belong**.

This yearning often drives our exploration, whether outwardly into the world or inwardly into our Souls. We are constantly looking for, longing for, something, something else, something more special, more exciting, more grandiose. We chase dreams and seek answers in the remotest corners, sometimes to satisfy curiosity but often to connect to something, to someone, or to ourselves. At its core, this longing is about being seen, heard, and loved, especially by those closest to us. Belonging is not just a desire; it is a fundamental human need. And maybe that's what makes us so beautifully human.

The human Circle of Belonging

Belonging is a circle – a space where we connect, contribute, and feel seen. At its core, it's the bond that ties us to one another, a reminder that we're never truly alone. This circle begins in the smallest of forms, with our families, our closest friends, or even one kindred Soul who seems to understand us. Over time, it expands to include communities, shared purposes, and the broader human family.

But here's the thing: The circle of belonging is not just something we join – it's something we create. When we let others in, when we offer recognition, love, or acceptance, we extend the circle. Every gesture of kindness, every moment of being truly present, strengthens it. And in return, we feel the warmth of being part of something bigger.

The beauty of this circle is that it's dynamic. It grows and shifts, sometimes breaking, sometimes mending. Yet, at its heart, it's a constant reminder of our shared humanity – our need to connect, to give, and to belong.

The ultimate Belonging

We all have a sense of limitless belonging to nature and the universe. Ultimately, **we belong to nature; we are nature**. We live the borrowed dust, moving creatures formed from clay and humus – this piece of matter we call our bodies. And yes, everything in today's life can be regarded as a constructed legal concept, a commercial contract. We set a legal label on everything and everyone – we construct and constrict. Somebody has ownership over something, and, in earlier days, even over someone. However, our self-constructed legal world of legal titles is indeed just a concept. We are all renters. Renters of natural resources, of our physical bodies. We are nature, and we give everything back to nature. When we all work together, it's a win-win-Win.

In a Nutshell

We all need to feel we belong – like we're seen, heard, and valued. It's not just a want; it's a need. Belonging gives you a sense of purpose, a place to rest, to be yourself. Without it, you feel untethered, adrift. But when you find it, even in small moments, it anchors you. It reminds you that you are not alone, that you matter, and that you are connected.

We close here with Mirabai Starr's contemporary translation of the beautiful words of St. Teresa of Avila:

There is a secret place, a radiant sanctuary,… constructed of the purest elements, overflowing with the ten thousand beautiful things, worlds within worlds, forest, rivers…bountiful forests, uni-

versal libraries,...this magnificent refuge is inside you,...enter, ...shatter the darkness that shrouds the doorway,...be brave and walk through the country of your heart.

Reflective Questions

1. When was a time you felt a deep sense of belonging? What made that moment special?
2. Have you ever felt like you didn't belong? How did that experience shape you?
3. What does belonging mean to you? How would you describe it in your own words?
4. Who in your life makes you feel like you truly belong? Why do you think they have that impact on you?
5. Do you think people need to feel a sense of belonging to live a fulfilling life? Why or why not?
6. How do you seek belonging in your daily life? Are there places or people that provide that for you?
7. What role does love play in your sense of belonging?
8. Do you think the need for belonging is universal, and do some people crave it more than others? Why?
9. How has your sense of belonging changed over time? Are there phases of life where it felt stronger or weaker?
10. What barriers have you faced in finding or maintaining a sense of belonging? How did you overcome them?
11. Do you think you must contribute to truly belong, or is it ok to simply take?
12. Do you always belong with the same Self or curate a different Self in different spaces?
13. What feels like home to you? When you are together with friends. When you are at your preferred place. When you feel your heart. When you do your preferred activity...

Wake-up Prompts for Belonging

1. John O'Donohue writes: *When you belong, it is as if you have come home to yourself, to a place of warmth, embrace, and integration.* How does this resonate with your experience? Write about a place or group where you felt completely at home, like you truly belonged. Paint the picture – what did it look, sound, and feel like?

2. Imagine a world where everyone feels a deep sense of belonging. What would that world look like? How would it feel different from the world today?

3. Create a character who has never felt like they belong. Describe their inner world and how they navigate relationships.

4. Write a letter to someone who made you feel like you belonged. What would you say to them?

5. Explore the idea of belonging through nature – how do animals, ecosystems, or seasons reflect a sense of connection and unity?

6. Describe the feeling of not belonging as if it were a physical place. What does it look like? What's it like to be there?

7. What does it mean to belong to yourself? Write about the journey of finding belonging within.

8. Imagine you've just joined a new community where you desperately want to belong. What steps do you take to connect with others? How do you feel along the way?

9. Write about the relationship between belonging and identity. How do they influence each other?

10. Create a poem or short story inspired by the phrase: »Longing for belonging.« And for thinking out of the box: Do you think we are self-domesticated apes?

CONTRIBUTION — Giving your Gifts to others

ˌkɒn.trɪˈbjuː.ʃən

⠐⠉⠕⠝⠞⠗⠊⠃⠥⠰⠎⠝

[from Latin *contribuere*: to bring together; to give or supply in common with others; give to a common fund or for a common purpose]

> When you cease to make a contribution,
> you begin to die.
> – *Eleanor Roosevelt*

Contribution (to contribute, contributing) – the altruistic act of giving from the heart or doing something to help achieve a common goal or purpose. Contribution is more than an action – it is the Soul's expression of love, compassion, and humanity. To contribute is to selflessly give a part of yourself, to reach beyond your own needs, and to touch the life of another. It is the thread that binds us together, weaving a tapestry of generosity, kindness, and shared purpose. Contribution and gift are like inseparable twins, born from the same Spirit of giving. Their closest companion? Generosity – the quiet, glowing friend that makes life rich and meaningful.

Every individual on Earth has a unique contribution, a special gift to share. When we truly contribute, we offer more than just help or resources; we give a piece of our heart. Whether it is a small gesture or a life-changing act, the impact of contribution ripples far beyond what the eye can see. In giving, we experience the beauty of connection. We soften. We feel the quiet peace of knowing we have made a difference, no matter how small. In giving, we grow. This act of reaching beyond ourselves brings fulfillment, meaning, and light to our lives.

The Magic of Giving

Why is it so important to contribute? Because we are human. Because we want to belong. Deep within us lies the desire to connect, to matter, to be a part of something greater than ourselves. Our hearts long for belonging, and through giving, we find it. We were not made to walk through this life alone. Contribution means *you are not alone. I am here with you.*

As we grow older, this longing deepens. We start to reflect on what we leave behind – the lessons, the memories, love. We realize that **life is** not **about** what we hold onto but **what we pass on**. We cannot take anything with us, but we can leave behind the gifts of our hearts: kindness, wisdom, and hope. This is how the circle of life completes itself – when we share what was so freely given to us by God, by the universe, by those who loved us first.

The act of giving is not just a learned behavior; it is a divine blessing passed down from those who nurtured us. From the unconditional love of our parents and caregivers, we learn to extend our hands to others. Their love echoes within us, reminding us that we, too, are capable of extraordinary kindness.

The Joy of receiving through giving

When we contribute, something magical happens. The more we give, the more we feel alive and happy. The more we share and serve to the greater good, the more we receive – not necessarily in material form, but in the deep and unshakable joy that comes from knowing we made a difference. Generous giving opens our hearts to gratitude, and gratitude fills our lives with abundance. It is a cycle as old as time: when we give freely, we receive tenfold in return.

The gift is to the giver, and comes back most to him – it cannot fail – Walt Whitman.

Through contribution, we light a candle in someone else's darkness. We offer a hand to lift them up. And in doing so, we discover that the light we bring to others illuminates our own path as well.

Speaking Contribution in your own Language

Impact – gift – donation – benefaction – the art of giving – offering – present – handout – generous – sharing & caring – I care about others – passing on – leave to – service to others – having a lasting nature in it – participation in – altruistic act – being actively engaged in life – betterment – benefits the community as a whole – volunteering – offering – to reach out a hand – helping – supporting – being of value – I am significant – I mean something to others – fostering a sense of compassion and empathy – …

To live and to leave a Mark of Love

Will you choose a life of ease, or a life of service and adventure? To contribute is to say, *I was here and made a difference.* Whether we give our time, our resources, or simply our compassion, the impact of our contribution lives on, echoing in the lives we touch. And as we share what we have been given, we honor the blessings that shaped us, ensuring they live on in the hearts of others.

Contribution is not just an act – it is a way of being. It is a promise to ourselves and the world that we will strive to be better, to love deeper, and to give without expecting anything in return. Because in the end, it is not what we take with us, but what we leave behind that truly matters.

So, **let us give**, not out of obligation but **out of love**. Let us contribute, not because we must, but because we can. And in doing so, may we discover the profound truth that to give is to live fully, deeply, and beautifully.

In a Nutshell

To contribute and make a difference is perhaps one of our deepest desires – to know our presence matters. This contribution can take infinite forms but stems from the same human need for significance. Contribution, in its essence, is the act of giving from the heart – a selfless expression of love and humanity. It fulfills our innate desire to connect, belong, and leave a meaningful mark. Through giving, whether time, resources, or compassion, we find peace, fulfillment, and purpose. Contribution fosters empathy, inspires others, and creates a ripple effect of kindness. As we share what we have been given, we honor the blessings in our lives and ignite a cycle of joy and gratitude. To contribute is to bring light to the world, leaving behind a treasure of love and generosity.

Reflective Questions

1. What does contribution mean to you personally?
2. What matters? And what matters most to you?
3. I heard the following question in a Podcast where Adam Grant discussed finding meaning in life, and it struck me. The question you should ask yourself related to contribution is: »Who would be worse off if I did not do my job / if I weren't playing this role?«
4. Can you recall a time when you made a meaningful contribution to someone's life? Think of all your contributions so far, no matter how small. It can be a smile to a stranger, your kids, or a friend. How did it impact both of you?
5. What would you like to contribute this month or year?
6. Do you see service to others as a way of life, a lifelong commitment?
7. Why do you think giving brings a sense of fulfillment and peace of mind?
8. How does generosity shape relationships and communities?
9. In what ways has someone's contribution impacted your life? How did it make you feel?
10. How can we teach the next generation the value of giving and contributing?
11. Are you choosing to live a story of significance?
12. Do you believe the best experiences are the ones shared with other people?

Wake-up Prompts for Contribution

1. Small acts of kindness and compassion: Remember that every contribution, no matter how small, can make a significant difference in somebody's life and the world. That's why you are now writing down three contributions you intend to make for the next week.
2. Describe a moment when contributing to a cause or helping someone brought you unexpected joy or clarity.
3. Write about how the desire to leave a legacy influences the way people give and share.
4. Explore the idea that *giving starts the receiving process*. Do you agree or disagree? Provide examples to espouse your perspective.
5. Imagine a world where every person commits to contributing in small but consistent ways. How would it transform our society?
6. Reflect on how contributing connects us to something greater, whether it's a spiritual belief, a community, or the whole world.
7. Discuss the emotional and spiritual rewards of giving compared to the material rewards of receiving.
8. Write about the lessons we learn about contribution from our parents, caregivers, or mentors.
9. Your time here on Earth is short – ask yourself: »How can I contribute beautifully?«

LOVE — The ultimate Connection
lʌv

⠇⠕⠧⠑

[from the Indo-European root *leubh*, meaning »to care,« »desire,« or »cherish«]

Life is the flower for which love is the honey.
– Victor Hugo

L: O∴ V∵ E∴ (to love, lovely) is such an intense force that it seems to permeate everything around us. Love is the highest power in the universe. It has the highest frequency and connects, unites, everything. It transforms everything it touches, and it touches everything. We are beings of love – born from it, sustained by it, and returning to it. Our very life force is activated by love. Love as the cycle of life – life as the loving cycle.

The heart as a symbol and ultimate expression of love is omnipresent. This deep connection between love and the heart is so profound that imagining one without the other feels impossible. Love awakens the youthfulness of the heart. What lifts your heart?

When your heart opens, it becomes a radical YES to life. Light shines through the cracks, the imperfections, and truths of the heart. True love isn't born from perfection but from embracing imperfection. When the outside light fades, your inner light glows brighter. Love arises from deep within – from the heart of hearts – bringing a soothing, boundless feeling. While the mind predicts, the heart breathes as expansively as the world.

Love is a complex and powerful emotion that binds people together while also having the capacity to cause heartache and pain. It is often described as an intense feeling of affection and attachment toward someone or something. Love is not merely a thought but an emotion felt deeply within the heart. It brings a sense of balance, peace, and contentment. Unlike other emotions that may feel dynamic or fleeting, love is settled, calm, and kind. It is more about being than doing – more about letting go than holding on.

Imagine the sun shining brightly all the time. At its center lies a living, peaceful resting point. The eyes form the portal to this vibrant stillness. Think of a baby's hearty laughter or the warm gaze of someone who has truly lived. The eyes are portals to the Soul, reflecting the heart's essence and connecting us to the Soul of another.

Love is the Foundation

We all crave love, acceptance, and validation. It's in our nature to want to belong, to fit in with our families, our communities, to the universe. When we open ourselves to this basic love awareness, good things just naturally flow into our lives. Even when everything else falls apart, love remains, gently reminding us that life is fundamentally good. And there's something about seeing the world through the lens of loving-kindness that makes us feel whole in a way nothing else can.

The Nature of Love

Love is both received and given; it flourishes in reciprocity. To me, the sun represents love – warm, radiant, and life-giving - while the moon embodies the Soul, mysterious and reflective, guiding us even in our darkest moments. It is intrinsically tied to peace, with each sustaining the other. Without love, peace cannot exist, and without peace, love cannot thrive. They are two sides of the same coin, interdependent and essential to one another. This inseparability underscores their shared role in fostering harmony and connection.

The remarkable aspect of love is its abundance: the more love we give, the more we find within ourselves. When we love, we engage our entire Being – our Souls turn toward the person or thing we cherish. At its core, **love is an act of surrender**, an attraction that draws us closer.

We will lose everyone we love. But love will always return in new forms. When you love someone, you will see their better Angel, their ideal higher Self. Encounter their humanity.

Sometimes, all it takes is a shift in perspective to recognize the love surrounding us. The love we seek exists everywhere, though we often fail to see it because we view the world through a clouded vision. The beloved we search for isn't confined to a single form – it's already spread throughout our world, manifesting in countless ways. In other words, the one is hidden in the many. When we learn to open our eyes, we discover that what we've been seeking has been present all along.

Various forms of Love

Love is a lived YES to belonging. It manifests in so many ways, each enriching our lives uniquely.

- **Romantic Love**: The deep affection, passion, and connection shared between partners. It is often accompanied by physical attraction, emotional intimacy, and a desire to nurture and support each other. Romantic love can provide a sense of belonging and partnership, making life's joys more profound and challenges more manageable.
- **Familial Love**: The unconditional love shared among family members. It is characterized by loyalty, care, and a sense of duty. Familial love forms the foundation of our early relationships and shapes how we connect with others throughout life. It provides a safety net of emotional support, fostering resilience and stability.
- **Platonic Love**: The deep bond of friendship and mutual respect that exists without romantic or sexual attraction. It is marked by trust, understanding, and shared experiences. Platonic relationships enrich our lives by offering companionship, personal growth, and a sense of community.
- **Devine Love**: The surrender to and connection with something greater than ourselves, such as a higher power, God, the universe, or spiritual beliefs. It is often described as unconditional, all-encompassing, and transcendent.

Love, in all its forms, is a fundamental human need that brings fulfillment, meaning, and joy to our lives. It's a declaration of boundless, wholehearted affirmation of our mutual belonging.

Empathy as a special Form of Love

Imagine truly seeing the world through someone else's eyes – not just stepping into their shoes but diving deep into their Soul. When we open ourselves to truly understanding another person's feelings, we build a connection that goes far beyond surface differences. It creates bridges of compassion and kindness, turning ordinary moments into meaningful exchanges. Empathy isn't just about reacting to someone's pain or joy; it's an act of love that heals, unites, and enriches our shared human experience.

Profound Moments of Love

Certain moments in life allow us to experience love in its depths and beauty, in transformative and unforgettable ways. Think of:
- the love a mother feels when giving birth.
- the deep connection and grief we feel when someone we cherish passes away.
- the unwavering love we show for our parents and friends during challenging times.

In these moments, love transcends the ordinary and reminds us of its intense capacity to connect, heal, and define our humanity. It reminds us of the profound goodness of every creature, of life itself.

Expanding Love

To expand our capacity for love, we must turn toward others and ourselves with intentionality and openness. Love does not require action so much as presence. However, in the distractions of daily life, we can lose sight of the love inherent in our relationships. Cultivating a loving-kind mantra or reflecting consciously on our thoughts and actions with a loving focus can help us rediscover and deepen our capacity for love. Intentionality in thought and action allows love to flourish and expand, enriching our lives and the lives of those around us.

Words of Love

Unconditional love → love without strings attached – parents – loving-kindness – live and love – lovable – Liebe zum Detail – l'amour – l'amour d'amitié – philia – shining – compassion – benediction – heart – feeling of gratitude – feeling of deep gratitude – warmth – blessings – sun – the fire in your heart – the eternal flame – newborn – Mother and her Baby – deep relationship – passionate activity – all-pervading – the fruit of the Spirit – rose – letting go and still feeling overwhelmed with blessings – Christmas – Peace – caring and concerning – a caring heart – energy that cherishes, protects and cares – Enlightenment – ignition of a light – golden light – warm light – the Source of the cosmos, of everything – all-encompassing light – the foundation of life – life itself – Resurrection – death – birth – le mois d'or – can lift us to the highest highs and sometimes bring us to our knees – binding us together – love is both longing and belonging – sanctuary – union – live openly – the seed from which everything grows – the higher purpose, crystallized, what remains – from soft like smiling or a helping hand to the grandest of sacrifices in giving their all for someone else's well-being

Love in several different Languages

Amor – Amore – Amour – Liebe – Liefde – Philia – Storge – Agape – Eros – Kärlek – Rakkaus – 爱 (Ài) – 愛 (Ai) – 사랑 (Sarang) – حب (Hubb) – Любовь (Lyubov) – Αγάπη (Agápi) – ความรัก (Khwamrak) – Tình yêu – Szerelem – Pag-ibig – אהבה (Ahava) – प्यार (Pyaar)

In a Nutshell

Love is too big to stay in a nutshell.

Just remember: If we have not learned or integrated any other life qualities, love can save us through everything. May the ears of your heart listen deeply to life!

Reflective Questions

1. Do you feel loved?
2. What does love mean to you?
3. In which moments do you experience deep love?
4. What does it mean to give love to another person?
5. Have you tried to expand your love level?
6. What is the color of love?
7. What does love taste/smell/sound like?
8. Live – Love – Matter: What does this mean to you?
9. Do you believe unconditional love exists? What happens when you look at your mother?

Wake-up Prompts

1. Visualize the word **love** for a while.
2. Manifest or meditate on the word love.
3. Imagine your love expands and try to feel it with every cell of your body.
4. Pen a heartfelt love letter to anyone or anything you love.
5. What do you think about the following statement: Attention is the most basic form of love?«
6. Tell everyone you love that you love her or him. You can speak it out loud or to yourself.
7. *Wisdom tells me I'm nothing. Love tells me I'm everything. And between the two, my life flows.* What does this quote by Nisargadatta Maharaj mean to you?

CONGRUENCY — Aligning your inner and outer Worlds

ˈkɒŋ.gruː.ən.si

⠀⠨⠀⠿⠿⠻⠨⠀⠐⠿⠀⠿

[from Latin *congruere*, »to come together,« »correspond with«]

> Happiness is when what you think,
> what you say, and what you do are in harmony.
> – *Mahatma Gandhi*

Congruency (congruent) refers at its core to the alignment between our thoughts, values, and actions. When these elements are in harmony, we feel authentic and better equipped to navigate life's complexities. In other words, **living in harmony with what we deep down know is consistently best for us**. This alignment helps build trust, foster meaningful connections, and develop a strong sense of Self. When I'm congruent, I experience life as coherent and consistent, allowing me to be myself genuinely.

The Language of Congruency

The language of congruency encompasses not just what you say but how you say it and the actions you take. In my experience, when we claim to value environmental conservation but consistently engage in wasteful habits, we send mixed signals. Our words and actions become incongruent, causing others to question our sincerity. You'll notice that tone of voice, body language, and facial expressions can either reinforce or undermine messages. We achieve authentic communication when our verbal and nonverbal cues align seamlessly with our intentions.

In relationships, congruency is crucial. When you apologize sincerely, it's not just through saying »I'm sorry,« but through a genuine tone, eye contact, and corrective actions. I've noticed that others perceive us as insincere if we apologize with defensive body language or a dismissive tone. Through personal experience, I've learned that our congruency in communication requires consistency across all channels of expression.

Why Congruency is Key

Congruency serves as the foundation for trust in our lives. When your actions consistently align with stated beliefs and promises, people develop confidence in your character and intentions. This trust is essential in both personal and professional relationships. In leadership roles, we inspire loyalty and respect when we »walk the talk« by embodying the principles we advocate. I've seen how incongruent behavior, like preaching collaboration while acting selfishly, can damage credibility and others' morale.

Congruency has become vital to personal fulfillment. When our actions align with our internal values, when we are living in accord with our inner reality, we experience a sense of coherence and integrity. You might have faced times when misalignment, like pursuing work that didn't match your passions, led to dissatisfaction and emotional discord.

In decision-making, congruency plays a crucial role. Aligning your choices with core values and priorities helps minimize regret and maintain clarity. For example, in pursuing a healthy lifestyle, we make decisions that align with our goals, like regular exercise and mindful eating, creating a positive feedback loop in our lives.

Aligning Actions with Thoughts

When our hearts and minds take different directions, life is difficult. Synchronization is needed to restore congruency.

The journey toward congruency requires constant introspection and deliberate effort. It begins with identifying your values, beliefs, and goals. Once these are clear, we should strive to align our thoughts and actions with these guiding principles. When you value honesty, you push yourself to communicate truthfully, even in challenging situations. I've found that consistency in this alignment builds integrity over time.

It is equally important to address incongruencies when they arise. Sometimes, actions or thoughts may stray from values due to external pressures or habits. Acknowledging these moments without judgment allows for realignment and growth. Techniques such as mindfulness and self-reflection can aid in recognizing these gaps and correcting them effectively.

In a Nutshell

Congruency is more than a personal virtue; it is a powerful force that underpins trust, authenticity, and self-fulfillment. By mastering the language of congruency and committing to alignment in thoughts, words, and actions, you can create a life that not only reflects your true Self but also inspires others to do the same. With this in mind, be congruent with the best of who you are – your best Self!

Reflective Questions

1. Does your life »make sense« to you? Do you think the different parts fit together?
2. Can you recall a recent situation where your actions did not align with your values? How did it make you feel?
3. How do you show congruency in your communication with others? Have you ever lost trust in someone because their actions didn't match their words? What did you learn from that experience?
4. When was the last time you felt completely authentic in a situation? What made it possible?
5. What specific habits or practices could help you align your thoughts, actions, and values more closely?
6. What steps can I take to align my current actions more closely with my long-term goals?

Wake-up Prompts for Congruency

1. **Journal prompt**: Write about a time when you felt truly congruent. What were you doing, and why did it feel so natural or fulfilling?

2. **Visualization prompt**: Imagine yourself living fully aligned with your values. Describe what your daily life looks like, the choices you make, and how you interact with others.

3. **Problem-solving prompt**: Think of an area in your life where you feel out of alignment. What steps can you take today to bring it closer to your true values?

4. **Role-model prompt**: Identify someone in your life (or a public figure) who exemplifies congruency. Write about how their alignment inspires you and what lessons you can apply to your own life.

5. **Action plan prompt**: List three specific actions you can take this week to ensure your decisions align with your core beliefs and goals.

Part IV: Creating Your Path

CURIOSITY — The Gateway to Possibility
ˌkjʊr.iˈɑː.sɪ.ti

[a strong desire to know or learn something, or an unusual or interesting object or fact]

> Miracles are only visible to those
> with eyes open to new learning –
> like the eyes of a child.
> – *Jonathan Robinson*

Curiosity (to be curious, curious) – this natural and profound skill we possess as humans plays a pivotal role in our personal growth. From the moment we are born, curiosity drives us – this inner force that makes a baby reach out to touch, taste, and explore the world. The instinct, this internal energy that drives a child to ask endless »why?« questions. While curiosity acts as an innate push factor, newness serves as the pull factor that attracts our curiosity. The German word for curiosity, *Neugierde*, literally »greed for newness«, captures this dual nature elegantly.

While it might seem simple, curiosity is actually one of the most vital skills a child can develop. Research shows that curiosity is one of the eight core abilities that shape successful, thriving kids (see Price-Mitchell, n.d.). When a child is curious, they're not just asking questions – they're unlocking the world, one discovery at a time. Through curiosity, they learn, grow, and build a **sense of wonder** that fuels their ability to explore and innovate. A curious child is more likely to become an adult who invents, questions, and creates. On the other hand, without nurturing this skill, a child may struggle to develop the mindset needed to embrace lifelong learning and growth.

Curiosity invigorates us and fills us with wonder. It makes the day enjoyable, turns it into an adventure. But what I have learned is that even though curiosity is innate, it's not something I can take for granted. It needs to be nurtured, encouraged, and celebrated.

Curiosity stands at the bridge between structured inquiry, science, and boundless imagination, art. Science asks how and why, while art explores what if. Together, they push boundaries, uncover new perspectives, and inspire innovation.

The Language of Curiosity

Curiosity feels like a whisper in our minds, nudging us to wonder, explore, and penetrate life's mysteries. It comes alive in the questions we ask, the small details we notice, and the connections we seek to understand. This language is playful and persistent, filled with questions like »Why?« »How?« and »What if?« -expressions that spark dialogue between ourselves and everything around us. It bridges gaps between disciplines, cultures, and generations, inviting us all to learn and grow. From a child's innocent »why« to a scientist's focused »how does this work?« the language of curiosity unites us, reminding us of our shared hunger to uncover meaning and discover the unknown.

What about the Curiosity of Adults

Curiosity doesn't fade as we grow older – but how we express it changes. For adults, being curious means actively seeking answers, asking questions, and diving deeper into the things that intrigue us. Unlike in childhood, where curiosity is often instinctive, adult curiosity is more intentional. It's a choice – a conscious effort to learn and grow.

When you embrace curiosity as an adult, to see the world through the eyes of a child, your mind becomes active rather than passive. That spark of inquiry strengthens your mental muscles, keeps your thoughts sharp, and expands your horizons. It inspires creativity, fuels innovation, and opens doors to new ideas and opportunities – the fountain of creation. More importantly, it plays a significant role in your personal growth, keeping life exciting, vibrant, and full of possibilities. It's also considered one of the most critical skills for future success.

Moreover, curiosity brings de**light**. It transforms the mundane into something magical, reminding us that life is full of mysteries waiting to be unraveled. What an incredible gift it is to be curious!

Are you a curious Person?

Everyone is curious, and each of us is an artist in their own way. We want to grow, experience new things. Curiosity is a fundamental human trait, our human Spirit, after all. But how curious are you? To find out, ask yourself:

- »Do I often ask 'Why?' questions, either out loud or in my head?«
- »Do I look up or research things that catch my attention?«
- »Have I gone out of my way to follow an interest or explore a subject simply because it fascinated me?«
- »Do I allow playfulness and joy?«
- »Do I set up for miracles to come and to embrace the newness of life?«

Reflecting on these questions can help you gauge your curiosity and understand how it shapes your perspective on the world.

Can you become more curious?

Absolutely! And here's the good news: Curiosity isn't a fixed trait. Whether you feel deeply curious or only slightly so, there's always room to grow. Developing your curiosity is about opening your mind – to have *un esprit ouvert*, »an open Spirit« – and allowing yourself to explore.

Start by consciously asking more »Why?« questions. Listen to that inner voice that urges you to dig deeper. Take note of what truly interests you, then dive into those topics with enthusiasm. Let yourself wander (and wonder) down new paths, even if they seem unrelated to your daily life.

When you make curiosity a habit – a way of life – you'll notice profound changes. You'll grow. You'll learn. And you'll find yourself rediscovering the excitement and wonder that makes life so extraordinary.

So go ahead, ask questions, explore, and let your curiosity guide you. It's one of the most powerful skills you'll ever have and yours to embrace.

In a Nutshell

Curiosity is your quiet learning guide, always asking, »Why?« and »What if?« It invites you to explore, connect, and understand the world. It has many layers – some spark quick questions, while others drive you to dive deep and uncover hidden truths. Whether it's about learning, feeling, or connecting with others, curiosity fuels growth, innovation, and a sense of wonder that keeps life exciting. Never stop pondering and asking questions. Embrace it, let it lead you – you never know what amazing discoveries are waiting.

Reflective Questions

1. What does curiosity mean to you? How curious do you think you are?
2. What's an area of your life where you've experienced deep curiosity? How has it influenced you?
3. How do you feed your curiosity? Have you tried it with playfulness and joy?
4. How can you make sure you never stop being curious?
5. How can we live with a more awakened curiosity?
6. When was the last time you let curiosity guide you into discovering something new? What was it, and how did it feel?
7. Do you think curiosity comes more naturally to children than adults? Why or why not?
8. Which question resonates with you more: »Why?« »How?« or »What if?« Why do you think that is?
9. Do you think curiosity is so restless that we cannot be at peace with the »state of the art«?

Wake-up Prompts for Curiosity

1. Go on a more prolonged nature walk and try to be more present with the environment. Try to immerse yourself in the specific environment's light, smells, and sounds. Later, back home, try to remember these feelings by taking five minutes to focus on the impressions you have experienced.
2. Describe a moment when asking »What if?« led you to an unexpected discovery.
3. Think about a time you bridged a gap between yourself and someone else through curiosity. What did you learn?
4. Write about how curiosity has shaped your understanding of a complex topic, emotion, or cultural experience.
5. Describe a moment when you moved from surface curiosity to deeper inquiry. How did it change your perspective?
6. Reflect on how curiosity has helped you challenge assumptions and discover something transformative.

INSPIRATION — Kindling the creative Flame
ˌɪn.spɪˈreɪ.ʃən
⠔⠔ ⠔⠔ ⠔⠔ ⠔⠔ ⠔⠔⠔⠔ ⠔ ⠔⠔ ⠔⠔ ⠔⠔

[**a:** the process of being mentally stimulated to do or feel something, especially to do something creative; **b:** or from the Latin *inspiratus*, the past participle of *inspirare*, »to breathe into,« »inspire,« and in English has had the meaning »the drawing of air into the lungs« since the middle of the 16th century or »the drawing in of breath«; «inhalation«]

> I aspire to inspire, till I expire.
> – *Les Brown*

Inspiration (to inspire, to be inspired, inspiring) has many faces. Wherever there is a will to live, there is inspiration, silently waiting to be seized by us. But it's easier to understand it as a process than a single word, as it's complex, elusive, and deeply personal. Each individual draws inspiration from unique sources. An opening inspirational question to ask is: *What has touched you to the depth of your Being?* Consider the following moments that often touch us deeply:

- Observing birds as they surrender to the air with grace
- Witnessing the dance of light and wind in the sky or stargazing, creating memory constellations
- Being fully absorbed in an engaging book or conversation
- Experiencing moments of stillness in nature – the power of silence
- Enjoying outdoor activities, whether on land or in water
- Countless other subtle experiences that spark silent inspiration

They allow us to feel life in all its depth and breadth and often fire our imagination. The Oxford English dictionary defines inspiration literally as »**the action, or an act, of breathing in or inhaling**. A **breathing in** or **infusion** of some idea, purpose, etc. into the mind: the suggestion, awakening, or creation of some feeling or impulse, especially of an exalted kind.« Wayne Dyer emphasized that inspiration arises from being *in-Spirit*, suggesting that by connecting to our higher Selves, we can transcend ordinary motivations and access a deeper sense of purpose. He stated, *when you are inspired by a great purpose, everything will begin to work for you.*

Inspiration is often spontaneous, like a spark waiting to be ignited. Once it lights up, it feels like pure bliss, absorbing us completely. It calls us to surrender to its pull. This alignment with something great(-er) amazes us. The flavor of inspiration commands our full attention – it feels miraculous, as if revealing something invisible, something between the tangible and intangible.

It's this interplay between our inner Selves and the outer world that creates the magic. When inspired, we immerse ourselves fully, merging with the environment, becoming one with the universe. Dormant forces within us awaken. When inspiration touches our hearts deeply, it can feel like a path to enlightenment.

Inspiration is our constant traveling companion. Each breath becomes a testament to the miraculous nature of existence. As spiritual beings in human bodies, we breathe in spiritual air and exhale gratitude, sensing a deep appreciation for life.

The Importance of Inspiration

Inspiration becomes even more significant when connected to other concepts, especially creativity. It serves as a powerful driver for realizing our creative potential, achieving goals, and enhancing well-being.

As Scott Barry Kaufman notes, *inspiration enhances motivation and brings ideas to fruition.* Writers, artists, and other creators have long argued that inspiration is a key driver of creativity. Over the past decade, scientific research has supported this view. Thrash and Elliot (2003) help us understand inspiration's unique characteristics:

- **Evocation**: Inspiration is evoked rather than intentionally initiated.
- **Transcendence**: It reveals new possibilities that go beyond the ordinary.
- **Approach Motivation**: It compels us to act, express, or bring new visions to life.

These characteristics distinguish inspiration from other mental states, highlighting its unique role in the creative process.

What inspires us?

Inspiration often arises from amazement, flow states, oneness, surrender, and deep immersion. When we experience profound awe, we are likely to feel inspired as well. While inspiration is deeply personal and varies widely, common triggers include:

- Time spent in nature, especially personal power places - in German *Kraftorte*. Maybe you have already tried what the Norwegians call *friluftsliv*, a simple life in nature without disturbing or destroying it. This concept is also tightly connected to *kos* or coziness, having a good time.
- Creative workflows
- Physical activity
- Any environment that stirs curiosity and sparks wonder

You'll recognize inspiration when you feel it – its presence is unmistakable.

> If you want to build a ship, don't drum up people to collect wood and don't assign them tasks and work, but rather teach them to long for the endless immensity of the sea.
> – *Antoine de Sint Exupéry.*

Creating inspiring Circumstances

While inspiration often seems spontaneous, it thrives when we actively create the right conditions. Personal effort is key; taking intentional steps toward your aspirations invites inspiration into your life. Exposing yourself to environments or activities that resonate with you supports this process. In other words, inspiration often stems from exploration; we don't invent something from nothing but uncover what already exists, like the discovery of gravity. In activating our potential, tapping into the creative field, we bring something hidden into the visible realm.

Curiosity and attentiveness are excellent precursors to inspirational moments. By cultivating open-mindedness and actively engaging with what draws your interest, you can set the stage for inspiration. The right environment – whether physical or mental – plays a crucial role, supporting the alignment of your inner Self with external possibilities.

Ultimately, inspiration is both a gift and a journey. By creating the right circumstances and staying open to its presence, you allow its transformative power to guide you toward creativity, fulfillment, and connection.

Inspiration in a Nutshell

Inspiration invites me to explore the boundless landscape of human creativity. A profoundly personal and multifaceted experience, often sparked spontaneously by awe, nature, creativity, or moments of stillness. It bridges your inner world with the outer, awakening dormant potential and driving creativity, motivation, and well-being. While inspiration feels like a gift, it thrives when you actively create supportive environments, remain curious, and embrace open-mindedness. It's a profound force that transforms your experiences, aligns you with the universe, and fuels your journey toward creativity and fulfillment. What is your gift of inspiration?

Reflective Questions

1. What moves and inspires you the most in your daily life, and why? What do you find to be **mysterious** or **magical** about life?
2. Can you recall a specific moment when you felt deeply inspired? What triggered it?
3. How does inspiration impact your creativity or motivation?
4. Do you think inspiration is something we can actively seek, or does it happen naturally?
5. How do **awe** and **wonder** contribute to your sense of inspiration?

6. What role does your environment play in inspiring you?
7. Have you ever been inspired by someone else's creativity or actions? How did it affect you?
8. In what ways does being in nature influence your sense of inspiration?
9. How does inspiration feel to you – mentally, emotionally, or physically?
10. What habits or practices help you stay open to inspiration in your life?

Wake-up Prompts

1. Describe a time when you felt completely absorbed by something inspiring. What was the experience like?
2. Write about the connection between inspiration and creativity in your own life.
3. Reflect on how moments of stillness or quiet have sparked inspiration for you.
4. Explore the relationship between inspiration and gratitude in your daily routine.
5. Imagine your ideal environment for fostering inspiration. What does it look, sound, and feel like?
6. Write about how a small, unexpected moment of inspiration changed your perspective.
7. Reflect on how inspiration has helped you overcome challenges or take meaningful action.
8. Create a list of activities or environments that make you feel most inspired.
9. Think about a person or piece of art that inspires you. What qualities stand out?
10. Write about the role of curiosity in finding and nurturing inspiration.

PASSION — Finding what moves you

'pæʃən

⠏⠈⠀⠏⠲⠏⠲⠲⠏

[**a:** to suffer, to be acted on; **b:** strong and barely controllable emotion; a strong feeling of enthusiasm or excitement for something or about doing something]

> Nothing great in the world has ever been accomplished without passion.
> – *Georg Wilhelm Friedrich Hegel*

Passion (being passionate about, passionately) – that feeling when your heart races and your whole being lights up with excitement. This incredible force that makes us pour our entire selves into something, even when it's challenging. This activity that feeds your heart and Soul. **The fire of aliveness**. It's fascinating how this profound emotion emerges most powerfully each Easter, when we witness the ultimate expression of passionate sacrifice: Jesus's journey. His suffering for humanity, taking away our sins, shows us what it truly means to be driven by something greater than ourselves. To put it differently, **worthwhile dreams and goals need effort and sacrifice to have personal meaning**. Or in the language of a rose: without thorns, there would be no roses.

In German, passion is expressed with the word *Leidenschaft*, where »suffering« is directly contained in the word. This suggests that only through personal, authentic suffering – meaning wholehearted – can genuine excitement and passion emerge. And to be honest, the most difficult experiences, those encounters with the Soul, were often the most developmental.

I am referring here to harmonious passion as opposed to obsessive passion, even though the distinction can often be fluid. I see harmonious passion as a conscious and balanced passion, in contrast to obsessive passion, where one is unconsciously or entirely consumed by an addictive drive.

The emotional Language of Passion

Imagine that **fire in your Soul** that burns so bright it lights up even your darkest moments – that's when the Soul of significance, passion, speaks. It's that mysterious force that whispers »keep going« when every fiber of your Being wants to give up. Like an endless **wellspring of energy**, passion fuels us beyond what we thought possible, pushing us forward not just because we have to, but because something deep within us needs to see our dreams come alive.

When I pursue one of my passions, for example, running outdoors, I usually feel truly alive. It's as if my passion breathes life into my existence. When passion flows through me, magic happens. My whole being tingles with an almost electric energy – mind, body, and Spirit dancing in perfect harmony. Time seems to melt away as I lose myself in those precious moments of pure joy and purpose. It's like catching lightning in a bottle, that sweet rush of fulfillment that makes me feel truly, intensely alive. In these moments, I'm not just performing at my best; I'm experiencing life in its purest, most vibrant form.

And then there's compassion – passion's gentle sister. *Com-passion*, meaning »to suffer together,« is that heart-swelling feeling when we reach out to others, connecting Soul to Soul with our fellow travelers on life's journey. This idea is deeply rooted in biblical teachings: *To love is to suffer, to suffer for and with others.* It's in these moments of shared joy and pain that we discover the deepest meaning of what it means to be human. When we open our hearts to others' struggles and triumphs, our own passion takes on new depth and meaning, weaving us all together in this grand tapestry of life.

How do we elicit Passion?

Passion doesn't simply find us; we discover it by living and choosing how we want to live. It exists within us but must be aroused. When we embrace new situations and adventures that evoke something novel in us, we can express ourselves creatively. This seeking of novelty and space for creativity is crucial for finding our passion and living an inspiring life.

When someone is passionate, you can feel their energy because it's palpable and infectious. They are on a loving path, and their energy seems to be on another level. They have heightened emotions and experiences, and that brings magic with it.

John C. Maxwell suggests three key questions that indicate a vibrant life:

- *What do you **sing** about?* ⊠ What makes you happy
- *What do you **dream** about?* ⊠ What would you like to be
- *What do you **cry** about?* ⊠ What hurts you, and you still love to do it

When living passionately, we often inspire others through our emotions and actions, helping them discover their own passion or contemplate it more deeply.

Moreover, passion affects us physically and emotionally – it makes our heart beat faster during intense moments (and slower during relaxation), energizes us, and often forms the foundation of an excellence-driven life.

Passion reminds us that everything in Life involves Effort

Don't we often want to get things done or receive material goods and accolades as soon as possible? We often seek quick results and immediate gratification, viewing the easy path as most desirable. However, as Les Brown notes, *if you do what's easy, your life will be hard. If you do what's hard, your life will be easy.* Choosing the easy way might benefit us in the short term, but it costs more in the long run. Additionally, it provides less satisfaction than accomplishing something valuable through effort.

People typically overestimate what they can achieve in the short run but underestimate their long-term potential. »Active patience« offers a solution: being patient while executing consistently, knowing that consistency compounds over time.

Living passionately and consistently guides us toward our destiny, which connects to our roots. Our heart knows what satisfies it and what it's willing to sacrifice for. Make a strong commitment and follow your passion – avoiding this path leads to regret.

Remember: everything great has been accomplished with passion. Uncover yours and express it.

In a Nutshell

Passion - this transformative force that gives life meaning through both joy and challenge. Like a rose with its thorns, passion involves the willingness to endure hardship for what we value most. We have to **find the gift in the pain**. Whether exemplified in Jesus's sacrifice at Easter or our personal pursuits, passion fuels us beyond our perceived limits and connects us deeply with others through compassion. It isn't something that simply finds us; rather, it awakens us as we actively engage with life, chase new experiences, and commit to what truly matters to us. When we live passionately, we not only reach our own peak experiences but often inspire others to discover their own path of purpose and meaning.

What puts a sparkle in your eyes? What matters so much to you that it completely consumes you, endeavors you? Something that you love so much that it kills you? Put your heart into it!

Reflective Questions

1. What are you passionate about? What feels **magnetic** to you?
2. What comes naturally to you? What feels effortless? What is your unique element that makes time disappear for you? What elevates your Spirit?
3. Do you have a preference for something?
4. What do you think about every day? What does your heart long for?
5. What is the activity you can't imagine living without? For what would you give almost everything?
6. What are you driven by?
7. What makes you feel alive? What is the difference between Aliveness and Passion?
8. Can you assert that you have almost died if you can't do it any longer?

9. What are you suffering for so that you feel better?
10. When did you last feel so passionate about something that time seemed to disappear? What were you doing?

Wake-up Call for Passion

1. *Like a rose and its thorns...* Write about a time when the challenges you faced while pursuing your passion made the achievement even more meaningful.
2. Describe a moment when someone else's passion inspired you to take action or think differently about your own life.
3. If your passion could speak, what would it say to your fears and doubts?
4. *Everything great has been accomplished with passion.* Share a story that proves or challenges this statement.
5. How has your understanding of passion evolved from seeing it as pure excitement to recognizing its connection with sacrifice and dedication?
6. Describe how compassion and passion intertwine in your life experiences.
7. Imagine your most passionate future self. What daily habits and choices led you there?
8. Write a letter to yourself about why your passion matters – not just to you but to the world.
9. *Find something you like to do so much that you would gladly do it for nothing; then learn to do it so well that people are happy to pay you for it.* What is your perspective on this quote from John C. Maxwell?
10. *The passionate heart never ages.* What does this note by John O'Donohue mean to you?

DREAMS — Envisioning your possible Future

driːmz
ˑˑːˑˑ ˑˑ ˑ

[**a:** a series of thoughts, images, and sensations occurring in a person's mind during sleep;
b: a cherished aspiration, ambition, or ideal]

> Dream as if you'll live forever.
> Live as if you'll die today.
> – *James Dean*

Dreams (to dream, dreaming) – one of life's most fascinating mysteries. Mysteries we spend moons of our lives with. They can feel like wild adventures, full of color and meaning, or slip away like a whisper the moment you wake up. Some believe dreams hold profound truths about who we are, reflecting our hidden thoughts, emotions, and desires – **narratives of desires**. Others see them as the brain's way of organizing itself while we rest. Whatever you believe, dreams have a way of touching something deep inside us, stirring curiosity and wonder.

The closest relatives of dreams are visions. They differ subtly: dreams flow through my sleep and hopes, while visions sharpen into clear mental images and personal aspirations. Both concepts are time-dependent, meaning they incorporate all our experiences. However, dreams are broader, encompassing the processing of the past and the hopes of the future, while visions focus on the future.

I often recognize my past dreams in my sleep. Dreams that are disguised as demons. They frequently appear in my dreams and want to tell and teach me something. And sometimes they come for several nights. I identify unfulfilled wishes in them. They haunt me, which means not all my dreams are so profound, but each one is a clue to what my Soul is processing. They speak to me, confront me with my unlived life – the denied permission to live a free journey. Even, or precisely because of, the seemingly mundane or bizarre dreams carry fragments of insight – **whispers from deeper parts of myself**.

The Language of Dreams

Dreams and visions speak the same language – **the language of imagination**. It's a language of symbols, emotions, and metaphors. In this world, a bird isn't just a bird; it could be your longing for freedom, your fear of heights, or the fleeting nature of joy. Dreams don't rely on logic or grammar but weave their stories through images that evoke feelings, memories, and instincts.

The same dream can whisper something entirely different to two people. A storm might represent chaos to one and renewal to another. This ambiguity is part of their magic: they invite you to interpret, to dive deep into yourself, and to find meaning in the fragments. To understand dreams, you don't decode them with rules – you feel them. Dreams speak from your heart to your Soul; sometimes, their message is clearer than words ever could be.

The inner Landscape of Dreams – How can Dreams help you live a more meaningful Life?

In dreams, the subconscious speaks to you, expresses itself, and gives clues. Dreams aren't just random images – they can be a powerful window into the Soul. Dreams weave the stories our desires tell.

Understanding the inner landscape of dreams can help you with self-reflection, emotional processing, and even creative exploration. By analyzing recurring themes and symbols, one can gain insight into personal challenges, desires, and mental states. Here's how they can make life richer and more intentional:

1. They reveal what's hidden inside you
Dreams often hold fragments of what you may not consciously see in yourself.
- That recurring dream about being lost or stuck? It might echo feelings of uncertainty in real life.
- A dream of flying could hint at your desire for freedom or confidence.

Reflecting on these symbolic stories can help you uncover your true desires, confront fears, and make sense of emotions you might not even realize you're carrying. In those quiet moments of understanding, you can feel closer to who you are at your core.

2. They spark Creativity (they bring more geist to zeit)
Dreams are pure imagination – unfiltered and limitless. Some of the world's most significant breakthroughs and works of art came from dreams:
- Mary Shelley dreamed up Frankenstein.
- Elias Howe, the sewing machine inventor, found the design in a dream.

Your dreams could hold the seed of a new idea, a fresh perspective, or an artistic vision waiting to come alive.

3. They help you solve and outgrow Problems
Have you ever woken up with a sudden aha-moment? That's because your mind keeps working while you sleep, untangling the knots of your day.
- A dream might present a creative solution to a challenge or give you clarity on something that felt impossible the night before.

Your subconscious mind whispers answers when your conscious mind gets out of the way.

4. They heal and guide you
Dreams can be a safe space to process emotions.
- Maybe a dream lets you reconnect with someone you've lost, bringing release and comfort.
- Or it helps you work through anxieties by playing out scenarios in a way that feels safe and distant.

When you pay attention to your dreams, you might find they gently nudge you toward healing and balance.

5. They can point you toward Purpose
Dreams have a way of asking questions we might avoid:

- Are you happy with where you're going?
- Are you chasing what truly matters to you?

A dream about missing a train or wandering aimlessly might be a sign to pause and reflect on your path. They can serve as little **wake-up calls**, urging you to live a life that feels meaningful and true to who you are.

How to embrace the Power of your Dreams

Dreams are like whispers from the parts of yourself you don't always hear during the day. By listening to them, you might find they have more to offer than you ever imagined. Here are some ways to catch your dreams:

- **Keep a Dream Journal**: Write down even the smallest fragments of dreams as soon as you wake up. Over time, you might notice patterns that surprise you.
- **Explore their Meaning**: Don't dismiss a strange or vivid dream – ask yourself, »What could this mean for me?«
- **Let them inspire you**: Whether it's a new idea, a story, or simply a fresh outlook, let your dreams fuel your waking life.
- **Be open to possibilities**: Sometimes dreams don't make sense right away, but they might hold meaning that unfolds with time.

Read your dreams. What are they trying to tell you?

In a Nutshell

Delay no time, defers have dangerous ends. I hope the words of William Shakespeare resonate in your ears as well. Your dreams are **whispers from your deepest parts**, speaking in symbols and emotions that words can't always capture. They take you beyond the limits of time and space into realms where anything is possible. When you pay attention to them, they can reveal hidden truths, spark your creativity, and guide you toward living a more intentional, meaningful life. Your dreams aren't just fleeting moments – they're gifts, inviting you to explore the vastness of who you are.

Be a dreamcatcher. Don't live your fears but your dreams, your true potential. So, resurrect your dreams, go wholeheartedly, and speak your dreams into existence. Remember the words of Eleanor Roosevelt: *The future belongs to those who believe in the beauty of their dreams.* I hope your dreams happen twice: first within your mind, and then without, in the »real« world!

Reflective Questions

1. What was your most exciting dream ever? Have you had any interesting dreams lately?
2. Do you remember what you dream about?
3. Are you daydreaming?
4. What recurring dreams or symbols have you noticed, and what might they mean to you?
5. Have you ever had a dream that left you with a strong emotion when you woke up? What do you think it was trying to tell you?
6. Is there a dream you've never forgotten? Why do you think it stayed with you?
7. Have you ever solved a problem or gained clarity about something after dreaming?
8. Do your dreams ever reflect themes or feelings from your daily life? How closely do they align?
9. Do you live out of your imagination?
10. Have you written out your dreams?
11. Do you think we were dreamed of for a long time before we were born?
12. What are you willing to do and endure to see your dream become a reality?

Wake-up Dream Prompts

1. Write your dreams on paper for the next couple of days and see how they inspire you.
2. Write down your most vivid dream and describe how it made you feel. What emotions or ideas come to mind as you reflect on it?
3. Write down five reasons why you deserve them. After you have written it down, commit and say to yourself: *No matter how bad it is or how bad it gets, I'm going to make it!*
4. Imagine your dream world as a place you visit every night. What kind of person are you in that world? What can it teach you?
5. Think about a dream where you felt free or powerful. How can you bring that feeling into your waking life?
6. If your latest dream were a message from your subconscious, what would you think it's trying to tell you?
7. Picture a recurring symbol or image from your dreams. What does it remind you of in your waking life, and what meaning could it hold?
8. Does the dream make the person or the person make the dream?

GOALS — Turning Dreams into Destinations

goʊlz

∷⠒⠄ ⠐⠂

[the object of a person's ambition or effort; an aim or desired result]

> Setting goals is the first step in turning the invisible into the visible.
> – *Tony Robbins*

G oals (to aim, aiming) – the objectives we aspire to achieve, guiding us like a compass toward the life we envision. They are more than just wishful thinking or tasks – they are the dreams we bring to life, the stepping stones that lead us more likely to fulfillment and success. We can think of goals as *dreams with a deadline*, guiding us toward the life we truly desire.

Why do Goals matter?

The beauty of setting goals is that they keep us focused and provide us with clarity and purpose. When we know what we're striving for, when we have a clear goal in mind, we can channel our energy and stay motivated, even when challenges arise. Goals serve as reminders of what's important and help us measure our progress over time, giving us a sense of accomplishment and pride.

The process of setting and pursuing meaningful goals is transformative. It helps us to unlock the potential within ourselves to live a more fulfilling and impactful life. They push us to learn new skills, develop better habits, gain insights that shape who we are. Whether it's a career milestone, a healthier lifestyle, or deeper relationships. Goals give us direction, helping us to grow, develop, and live a life that feels intentional and rewarding. Achieving our goals is deeply satisfying, but the journey itself is just as valuable, teaching us resilience, patience, and determination. Each small win builds confidence, and even setbacks teach us valuable lessons.

The Power of smart Goals

Goals have many different faces, reflecting our diverse ambitions and priorities: Whether we're aiming to advance our career, improve our health, build stronger relationships, or grow personally, goals give us something concrete to work toward. To make these goals truly effective, it helps to make them **SMART**:

- Specific: Clearly define what you want to achieve.
- Measurable: Track progress and celebrate milestones.
- Achievable: Set challenging but realistic and attainable targets.
- Relevant: Ensure your goals align with your broader aspirations.
- Time-bound: Give yourself a timeline to stay focused and motivated.

This turns vague wishes into actionable plans. It's the difference between saying *I want to be healthier* and *I'll walk for half an hour every morning before work.*

Goals as a Gravity Point

A good goal doesn't mean chasing after more or achieving as much as possible. Instead, it's about freeing yourself from the trap of always wanting more. Sometimes, doing less allows you to achieve more in meaningful ways. Quality goals are about **intentionality** – they are **non-negotiable commitments** to yourself.

Remember, when you invest time and effort into working on your goals, they also work on you. Like magnets, they draw you closer with every step you take. They shape your mindset, help you grow, and transform you into the person you want to become. By prioritizing quality over quantity, you create space for clarity, progress, and fulfillment.

In a Nutshell

Goals are the objectives we strive for, guiding us toward a purposeful and fulfilling life. They **provide direction**, **motivation**, and a way to measure progress while fostering personal **growth**. By setting clear, meaningful goals, you turn your dreams into actionable steps, shaping both your achievements and the person you become.

So, take that first step - transform your aspirations from »someday« dreams into »today« actions. Pursue them with clear intention. They're not just tasks on a to-do list; they're the decisive points on the map to a life filled with purpose, growth, and joy.

Reflective Questions

1. What worthy idea and goal do you have?
2. Have you set goals for the day, week, month, year, or years to come?
3. Do your goals fit the person you are, and are they the best for the person you hope to become?
4. Do you write your meaningful goals on paper?
5. What does achieving your goals mean to you, and how has and will it change your life?
6. When was the last time you felt genuinely proud of accomplishing something? What did that teach you about yourself?
7. Are there any dreams you've put aside? What would it take to revisit them?
8. What challenges have prevented you from pursuing your goals, and how can you overcome them?
9. How would you feel a year from now if you started working toward a meaningful goal today?
10. Why does the goal(s) matter to you? What will achieving your goal(s) do for you?

Wake-up Prompts to achieve your Goals

1. Write down your three most important goals that truly excite you and why they matter to you.
2. Imagine your ideal life five years from now. What goals would make that vision possible?
3. Think of one concrete step you can take to take you toward your goal. Can you do anything that might bring you closer to your goals?
4. Write about a time you faced an obstacle but kept going. How did it feel to push through, and what did you learn?
5. Describe a goal you've achieved in the past. What steps did you take to make it happen, and how did it feel to succeed?
6. If there were no limits – time, money, or fear – what goal would you pursue, and why?

Part V: The Journey of Manifestation

ACTION — Moving from Thought to Reality

ækʃən

⠈ ⠶⠰⠾⠈⠐⠰⠾

[*agere*, »to do« or »to act«]

> You are what you do, not
> what you say you'll do.
> – *Carl Jung*

Action (to act, to activate, actionable) breathes life into thoughts and concepts. It is **the rhythm of progress, the pulse of creation**. We all have countless ideas swirling in our minds, yet they only gain significance when put into motion. Visions and dreams, like shadows, remain intangible unless pursued with unwavering determination. Even the smallest act, like planting a seed, holds profound potential for transformation; for within that act lies the promise of growth, change, and the unfolding of what could be. And this is what we yearn for: real experiences, an adventurous life where we immerse ourselves in the cosmic dance of the universe, nature's language.

Even the smallest, most imperfect actions reverberate with a truth that words alone cannot convey. They are **tangible manifestations of our intentions**, quiet yet powerful sparks that ignite momentum, and the unseen currents that inspire transformation. Action does not seek the comfort of perfection; instead, it calls for more profound virtues, the courage to confront the unknown, the commitment to honor purpose, and the persistence to weave progress from the threads of imperfection.

Challenges will undoubtedly arise along the way, and guess what, they are essential catalysts for growth. To truly evolve, we must venture beyond familiar paths, beyond the beaten paths, and embrace discomfort. No pain, no gain. This process of positive dis-integration, where our former Selves break down, creates space for a higher version of ourselves. Like a caterpillar dissolving in its cocoon before becoming a butterfly, transformation requires us to let go of who we were to become who we can be.

The Language of Action

Actions speak a language that words can never quite match. They are honest, unfiltered, and undeniable. While words can promise, excuse, justify, or embellish, actions lay everything bare – they reveal what we truly value, what we're willing to commit to, and what we stand for.

The language of action is universal. There is no need for explanation when you show up for a friend, chase a goal, or make a bold move. People understand who you are by observing what you do. This language is intricately woven into the tapestry of our lives, shaping relationships, building trust, and defining success.

However, taking action requires intention and courage. It involves moving beyond hesitation, silencing doubt, and proving through effort that our desire is genuine. Actions not only communicate with others – they speak to us, reinforcing our beliefs and molding our identities.

Every action we take is a sentence in the story of our lives. So, it is crucial to choose your actions wisely because, in the end, our actions will dictate **how our story turns out**. In other words, what you do will always say more than what you intended to do.

Why does Action often feel difficult?

Embarking on an action can feel so much more challenging than it truly is, even when our desires are sincere and our intentions clear. Why is this the case? Fear may play a role – fear of failure, fear of inadequacy, fear of disappointment. At times, we tend to overthink everything – we endlessly procrastinate, magnifying the task at hand and making it appear more daunting than it actually is. We convince ourselves that we must wait for the »perfect moment«, but deep down, we understand that such a moment may never arrive. Let's be honest – staying in our comfort zone often feels safer than stepping into the unknown.

But here's the thing: the most challenging part is simply starting. The moment we take that first small step, the journey feels easier. We realized the seemingly insurmountable task wasn't as impossible as we had imagined. And what's more, action is the catalyst that turns dreams into reality. So even if it feels hard, trust yourself enough to start. You'll be glad you did.

Action as a Catalyst

The most powerful message? It's the one you actually live. Let's be honest – we don't really know what we want, who we are, or how change feels until we've gone through it ourselves. That's why taking action – just that next right step that aligns with your values – matters so much.

When you act, especially on what truly matters, you create magic. It's the **super-connecter** to all other ingredients, the bridge between your intentions and the impact you desire to build in the world. Every deliberate step you take solidifies the bridge between your dreams and the tangible outcomes you seek. And the more you put yourself into what you're doing, the more fully you engage with your efforts, the more significant difference you'll make.

But it goes beyond just you, beyond individual progress. Your actions create waves that energize everything around you and light a fire under others. When you move with real purpose, that energy is contagious. Once it's out, it changes the whole environment. People respond differently when they feel the authentic power behind your actions.

Building Momentum through Action

Remember the quote by John Bytheway, *Inch by inch, life's a cinch?* Or, *little by little becomes a lot?* We build momentum each time we execute against those little things that really add up. Repetition strengthens action. Each step, no matter how tiny, reinforces a habit, etching new pathways into your subconscious mind. Over time, the initial effort evolves into a natural pull, a tr-action, propelling you forward with ease. What begins as a deliberate effort becomes instinctual, turning intentions into a lifestyle of consistent action until it becomes a point of no return, your destiny.

High-quality Actions

Not every action goes in the right direction. Don't let yourself be trapped by moody feelings and distracted moves. What I do not mean are actions that bring sand to the beach. What I mean are needle movers. The actions that really drive us, bring us joy, meaning, and fulfillment.

Imperfection as a Strength

Action is beautifully imperfect, and that's its greatest strength. Each step, no matter how small, is a declaration of growth, resilience, and aliveness. Yes, sometimes you have to take two steps back for every step forward. Success is not born from getting it right the first time but from showing up time and again, learning through experience, and refusing to quit. I personally take success with a healthy dose of self-irony. For me, success was always something strange. When it supposedly materialized, I asked myself, *how did I manage that? I didn't do anything?* At least, that's how it felt. The irony of the story? At some point, success comes by itself...

Benefits of taking Action

Alignment: Action bridges the gap between your inner desires and external reality, fostering a sense of harmony and fulfillment.
Understanding: We have to live our set intentions so that we receive feedback, even if it doesn't always seem to be in our best interests at first glance. True understanding emerges through doing; understanding-by-doing. Experience is the ultimate teacher.

Creativity: Action sparks creativity. We discover new things, which in turn stimulate new ideas.

Courage: Stepping into the unknown strengthens your courage and opens doors to uncharted opportunities.

Positivity: By acting, we can direct our feelings in a preferred way. Positive actions create positive outcomes, uplifting both your emotions and mindset.

Fulfillment: Life rewards those who act. Fulfillment comes from knowing you've given your all, regardless of the outcome.

Daily Priming for Action

Consistent action begins with consistent intentions. Challenges and setbacks will arise along the way. But all challenges are pregnant with opportunities. See the opportunity in every disruption. Or reframe your perspective on them. When you see them as teachings, as learning lessons, as sacraments rather than as sacrifices, you mentally prepare, you prime yourself for acting, no matter what.

Start your day by priming yourself:

- **Reflect** on your core goals and values.
- **Write** down your key intentions for the day.
- **Visualize** yourself by taking meaningful steps toward your vision. Break it into small steps so that you can digest it more easily.

And don't forget to repeat this priming process because we forget quickly. The more we prime and the more often we repeat, the more it can become a habit that sticks.

In a Nutshell

The path to a meaningful life is paved with action. The most effective message is the one you live. Each step, no matter how small, is an investment in your dreams and a declaration of your purpose. If you realize that hidden treasure in your heart, your inner and outer worlds feel aligned, and you become the person you are constantly dreaming of. Fulfillment belongs to the person who dares to act, who transforms intention into impact, and who embraces the journey of becoming the most whole Self.

Remember, it's doing, not thinking about doing, that creates a life worth living. Showing up – growing up – as best as we can, is all that life really demands of us. It's time to work out your dreams, time to bring your thoughts and manifestations into play. Let your actions speak and inspire the world!

Reflective Questions

1. Where do you need to grow up, step into your life?
2. What small action can you take today to move closer to your vision and dreams? Ask yourself: What is one thing I can do today to move closer to what I truly want?
3. How does your current field of action align with your aspirations?
4. What would you regret more: failing or never trying?
5. Who or what can support you in taking the first step?
6. What does bravery look like, and how can you embody it today?
7. Do you think action is the ultimate solution to regrets (the dissolver of *coulds, woulds, shoulds*)?
8. Do you think attitude follows action more often than action follows attitude? Why or why not?
9. Are your actions serving your mission and purpose in life?

Wake-up Prompts for Action

1. Reflect on the small, everyday actions that define your routines. Are they building the future you want?
2. Don't ask, »What will it cost me to act?« Instead, ask, »What will it cost me if I don't?«
3. Transition from thinking and planning to doing and showing.
4. Prime yourself daily: Write down your key intentions and take one actionable step every day.

5. Write about a time when your actions didn't align with your intentions or values. What did you learn from it?

6. Imagine someone observing your life without hearing you speak. What would your actions tell them about you?

7. Describe what the »language of action« means to you personally and how you've seen it shape your life or the lives of others.

8. What do you think about the following quote by Bill Wilson: *You can't think your way in the right direction, you have to act your way in the right thinking.*

EXPRESSION — Bringing your inner World outward

ɪkˈsprɛʃ(ə)n

⠈⠑⠈⠅⠈⠎⠏⠈⠗⠑⠈⠎

[the act of saying what you think or showing how you feel using words or actions]

> Make the impossible possible,
> the possible easy,
> the easy elegant.
> – *Moshé Feldenkrais*

Expression (express, expressive) or self-expression – whether through words, gestures, or art – is a beautiful act of **communication** that allows us to share our feelings, thoughts, and ideas **in unique ways**. It is creativity when we share our originality and innovation. Expression is creative when you let your heart truly speak. In this sense, creativity is a nuanced expression. Expression is pure, raw. We are living canvases. Even more so when we let our true selves out into the visible realm.

Expression is fundamental to human connection, enabling us to develop our identities and form deeper relationships with the world. Through self-expression, we transform our inner energy into something tangible, shaping the world and positively impacting ourselves and others. It's not so much what we communicate but how. We don't bring our world into fruition with what we do, but how we do. This is the significance behind our expressions.

Every human has their own style of showing up. This style reflects attitude – a more constant and stable core – while style itself is flexible, adaptable to circumstances, yet still true to the individual. In other words, everything that defines a person is expressed in an inner and an outer attitude.

The Art of Expression

We have absorbed and incorporated so much into our lives. We carry within us a lifetime of accumulated experiences. This inner collection longs for expression – it yearns to be released. Our inner wisdom is speaking, urging us to be heard.

Setting an intention for our expression is like choosing the lens through which we share ourselves with the world. It's not about wearing a mask to please others; it's about letting our inner light shine in its own unique way (I know, being entirely ourselves is more challenging than it sounds – impossible indeed). When we focus on authentic expression rather than impression, we transform our inner energy into something beautiful that touches others naturally.

One of the purest forms of self-expression I can imagine is dance. Dance exists at the intersection of music and movement, where emotions are translated into motion. A dancer can convey feelings delicately, with a beauty that words often cannot match.

Expression also manifests clearly in the face – a unique human canvas. From the first moments of life, babies display distinct and unmistakable facial expressions. These tiny gestures communicate individuality and emotion in ways that transcend words, reminding us of the innate nature of expression.

Axioms for Expression – Expression is...

Like a window to our Soul – the art of the Soul expressing itself – we can express what we really believe – each individual expresses and incarnates a different dimension of divinity – the expression of our heart – a glad heart wants to express – expressed in every dimension – expressing compassion – to express all possibilities – a unique expression of the true self, our inner nature – expressing our feelings – the power of presence naturally expressed in a baby's smile – every dimension of the face expresses presence – in dance, when the whole body becomes expressive – where a dancer painting emotions in the air – turning your inner music into a melody that others can hear – where every gesture tells a story – innovative, creative and expressive are very close neighbors – express it in different ways – a matter of life, not of definitions – impressionism as opposite or inclusion? – connecting on a deeper level – tapping into our innermost emotions – conveying thoughts and emotions – shaping the world – expressionism – revealing the inner world – what brings out the best of you – authenticity – to really be oneself – inner nature – dance – drawing – writing – your true and wild story – crafting – body awareness – gaze – magic that is uniquely me – movement – feelings – body language – vocalizing – singing – arts – mimic – gestures – letting your body speak – signature – personal brand – style – unique style – eccentric, idiosyncratic style – signature way of showing up – fingerprints of our Spirit – being true to your Self – universal language and most profound understanding – personal style.

Is the Awareness of Self-Expression helpful?

Being aware of our self-expression can be powerful for introspection and growth. It prompts us to ask: Who is the person behind the person? By exploring this, we uncover the many layers of personality we carry within us. Conscious self-expression, in its various forms, is not just about communicating to others – it is also about understanding ourselves. It opens doors to healing, growth, and authenticity.

The Power of authentic emotional Expression

Have you ever watched a baby's face? It's like watching pure emotion in its most honest form. One moment they're beaming with joy, their whole face lighting up like sunshine, and the next they might scrunch up their tiny features in curious confusion. Each expression is so pure, so real – it reminds us of how naturally expression flows when we're not overthinking it.

Expressing our emotions authentically is vital for well-being. When we become intentional, we build congruency about the message and energy we share, we naturally align with our true Selves. It is not about impressing others or suppressing what we feel; it's about expressing our truth with clarity and purpose.

While we all want to leave a positive impression, the real key lies in our focus. When our attention shifts toward authentic expression rather than external validation, we reveal our genuine nature. The result is not just personal clarity but also a sense of lightness and freedom as we transform our energy into the world in a way that feels honest and meaningful.

In a Nutshell – Call for Expression

Expression is how you take what's inside – your thoughts, feelings, and energy – and share it with the world. It's how you say, »This is me. This is what I feel.« Whether through words, art, movement, or even a look on your face, it's your way of connecting, of being seen, and of letting go. When you express yourself honestly, you are not just sharing – you are freeing a part of who you are and leaving something real behind. It's about showing up as you are and letting the world feel your truth.

Reflective Questions

1. What does expression mean to you? In which ways do you express your feelings?
2. Do you feel certain areas of your body where pain arises if you try to express your feelings? Are you withholding something from being fully expressed?
3. Do you feel certain areas of your body where you have a very releasing or joyful feeling when you express yourself? What forms of expression make you feel the most alive (e.g., writing, dancing, speaking, creating art)?
4. What comes to mind when you think of self-expression?
5. Are you aware of what your own unique signature style is? Can you describe it?
6. Do you feel especially connected to others when you communicate through your typical signature style?
7. Are you aware of your body language during the day? In which situations more? In which situations less?

8. When was the last time you expressed something that felt truly authentic? What was that experience like?
9. Which language(s) do you speak? The language of dance, singing, sport…?
10. What is the most honest and authentic expression of yourself?
11. What wishes to be expressed through you?

Wake-up Prompts for Expression

1. Express your feelings in a way that suits you.
2. Now tell someone about your feelings and try to express them differently.
3. How do you feel when you express them in different ways? Write those feelings down.
4. Now, think of one of your favorite activities. Imagine that you expand your unique self-expression through your favorite activity. How does it feel?
5. Create a dialogue where two people express their feelings through body language alone – no words allowed.
6. Imagine a world where emotions appear as colors around people. Describe how people express and hide their true Selves.
7. »If I could express myself without fear, I would…« Write about what you would do, say, or create if there were no fear of judgment.
8. »My unique style of expression looks like…« Describe how you communicate your personality, thoughts, and feelings. What makes you uniquely you?

MANIFESTATION — Creating your Reality
ˌmæn.ɪ.fɛsˈteɪ.ʃən
⠍⠁ ⠝⠊⠋⠑⠎⠞⠑⠌⠕⠝

[becoming visible or revealing of all kinds of things that were previously invisible or formless]

Nothing is impossible, the word itself says »I'm possible.«
– *Audrey Hepburn*

Manifestation (to manifest, manifesting) – the act of bringing something into existence or making it visible. It is often associated with the law of attraction and stems from the belief that positive thoughts and intentions can lead to desired outcomes. When we yearn for an experience, it shows up sooner or later. At its core, manifestation begins with desire – even the desire to be desireless is itself a desire.

Manifestation is tapping into your energy field, transforming potential into a tangible form or, more concisely, another form. It's not about creating something from nothing but rather aligning yourself with previously unknown or unaware aspects of yourself. As Wayne Dyer noted, you and what you wish to manifest are one – it already exists, just in a different form.

Harnessing the Power of Manifestations

Manifestation is better grasped by imagining it as a verb, an active process. We do something to get something out of it. The power of positive manifestations can be incredibly transformative. When we focus our thoughts and feelings on our goals, we create a roadmap for our future. This practice can boost self-esteem, reduce stress, improve relationships, increase motivation, and foster success across various areas of life. The key is maintaining an intentionally positive and hopeful mindset to attract abundance.

Remember, it first moves in your mind and then manifests in your body. Everything is manifested in your body. I believe your body is the image of your mind.

Forms of Manifestations

There are several approaches to manifestation, and there is no straight line between the various concepts. Common and powerful tools are:

- **Affirmations** are positive statements that challenge negative thoughts and beliefs and reinforce a positive attitude. They are a powerful tool that can be used to reprogram the mind and change negative thought patterns into positive ones. Positive affirmations help create a mindset focused on success, happiness, and abundance. The words we choose matter. By repeating affirmations regularly, one can create a positive, empowering belief system that supports one's goals and aspirations.
- **Contemplation** is a process of deep thinking and reflection. It involves focusing on a particular idea, situation, or problem, and exploring it from different angles to gain a deeper understanding. Contemplation can be a powerful tool for personal growth, as it allows us to develop insights and perspectives that we might not have considered before. Whether through meditation, journaling, or simply taking a quiet walk in nature, taking time to contemplate can help us connect with our inner selves and find greater clarity and purpose in our lives.
- **Mantra or** a short **Quote** – Words, phrases, or sounds repeated to aid concentration – can focus the mind and cultivate positive thoughts. Derived from Sanskrit, *man-tra* literally means »instrument of the mind.« Both mantras and powerful quotes, winged words, can serve as tools for meditation and personal affirmation.

Practice makes permanent

Manifestation brightens your worldview if you practice it every morning when you wake up or write it down in a journal before you go to sleep. The more you practice, the more likely it becomes a habit. So, unplug from all your unwanted conditional thinking and take on the challenge of manifesting your heart's desires into your destiny. In this way, you condition your mind with positive thoughts.

In a Nutshell

Manifestation is the practice of transforming desires and intentions into reality through focused positive thinking. It works through various approaches: affirmations (positive statements), contemplation (deep reflection), and mantras (repeated phrases). When practiced regularly as part of daily routines, manifestation can help improve various aspects of life, including self-esteem, relationships, and personal success. The key principle is that what we wish to manifest **already exists within us, waiting to be transformed into visible form.**

Reflective Questions

1. Do you have daily manifestations that lift your mood for the day?
2. Which form of manifestation do you practice, and how often?
3. How and where do you practice them? Why so?
4. How do you distinguish between wishful thinking and effective manifestation practices?
5. What role does action play in the manifestation process, beyond positive thinking?
6. Can you recall a time when you successfully manifested something in your life? What made it effective?

Wake-up Prompts

1. Surrender and go deep within you. Trust everything that comes up. Dream up your own uniquely inspiring phrase to say every day or let yourself be inspired by powerful quotes. Say it from your heart, say it simply, say it directly.
2. Look at your manifestation practices and try to live them

as often as you feel you need them, at least once a day. Focus on the positive!

3.   Write about three things you'd like to manifest in your life and why they matter to you.

4.   From »I want...« to »I am...love and loved, careful, alive, healthy, happy, free, creative, thankful. You are already connected to God.

5.   Ask yourself, »What if [positive statement]?«. For example, what if I reach my goal?

6.   Journal prompts:
     a.   »Today, I am grateful for...« (complete this statement focusing on what you already have)
     b.   »The version of myself I'm working to manifest is...« (describe in detail)
     c.   »One small step I can take today toward my goals is...«

7.   *Ask, and it will be given to you; seek and you will find; knock and the door will be opened to you. For everyone who asks receives; the one who seeks finds; and to the one who knocks, the door will be opened.* What does this Bible verse from Matthew mean to you?

8.   Complete the sentence as desired: I deserve to be (loved, embraced, cared for...) in every way I ever dreamed I could be.

Nothing can dim the **light** that **shines from within** – *Maya Angelou*

The emotion that can break your heart is sometimes the very one that heals it – Nicholas Sparks

The only courage you ever need is the courage to fulfill the dreams of your own life – Oprah

The ultimate truth of who you are is not I am this or I am that, but I Am – Eckhart Tolle

Your life is already a miracle of chance waiting for you to shape its destiny – Toni Morrison

We must accept finite disappointment, but never lose infinite hope – Martin Luther King Jr.

You must do the things you think you cannot do – Eleanor Roosevelt

When someone says you can't do it, do it twice, and take pictures – Unknown

Only the one who walks his own way can't be overtaken – Marlon Brando

Things you should **never forget**:

♥ Listen to your ♥!

♥ Trust your gut!

♥ You are stronger than you think you are!

♥ Life is beautiful – You are beautiful!

♥ Be open for change – be curious

♥ Each day is full of chances

♥ Go **YOUR** own way, it's the right one

♥ Never give up – things need time and they blossom when it is the right time

♥ Be thankful for all you get and love

♥ Have faith – believe in **YOU**!

♥ Luck will find you – be patient and laugh!

♥ Even the darkest night comes to an end – be patient!

♥ You have greatness in you!

♥ Do what you love and do it often!

♥ Even with small deeds you can bring great joy

♥ Befriend everything you get

♥ Let go of what's pulling you down

♥ Be kind to yourself – you are precious

♥ You are not everything, but everything is nothing without **YOU**!

♥ Wonderful moments often come unexpectedly

♥ Count on everything

♥ There are no failures, just learnings!

♥ Treat yourself to a break!

♥ Remember – **YOU** are a wonderful being

♥ If you can dream it, you can do it

♥ Live, love, and laugh wholeheartedly

MISSION — Your exceptional Difference-Making

ˈmɪʃən
⠍⠊⠎⠎⠊⠕⠝

[from Latin *missiō* (genitive: *missionis*), meaning »the act of sending« or »a dispatch«; derived from the verb *mittō, mittere, mīsī, missum*, meaning »to send« or »to let go«; over time, the meaning expanded beyond religious contexts to include any significant task or purpose someone is »sent« to accomplish]

> Every person above the ordinary has a certain mission that they are called to fulfill.
> – *Johann Wolfgang von Goethe*

Mission (to mission, missionary, or missioned) bridges the gap between your vision, your higher, primary calling, and your individual objectives. It acts as a guide, showing the way to achieve your overarching goals, fulfilling your purposes. In daily life, your mission provides direction and helps align your actions with your personal values and priorities.

Like a compass, a mission offers clarity on how to achieve your goals. It connects your vision and purpose to the mundane, giving your vision actionable steps and traction. When you declare your vow to a beautiful idea, when you make a promise to make good on the vision, you are mapping out your future. In other words, when **imagination meets determination**, you become unstoppable.

With a clear mission in mind, **your destination becomes your destiny**. A mission is more than just an action – it's a vocation, a personal philosophy, a creed. A massive, purposeful movement. When you are on a mission, you are unstoppable. You know precisely what you are doing and take consistent action, over and over again. A mission is not just a goal; it's an internalized direction, an embodied purpose. It's lived, not just known, until it becomes second nature – a habit, a way of being.

When I'm on a clear mission, I feel so much better – relieved.

A feeling of full commitment and complete relief at the same time. It drives me to bold action. **I get what I must have**, not »shoulda-woulda-coulda-s.« I'm trying again and again. **I am trying until!** No force can divert me from my chosen direction. Nothing can knock me down. It's a lifelong process. People will listen; in fact, they already listen. Others follow **the path of the strongest conviction**. I am the first to move and the last to stand. **Aim – Ready – Fire**.

Why a Mission Statement matters

A well-defined mission statement articulates the essence of your vision. It serves as a reminder of how you aim to achieve your (overarching) goals and ensures you stay focused on what truly matters. Even if you're uncertain about your life's purpose, a mission statement can help clarify your vision and guide your actions. It helps you to determine what to say **yes to** and what to say no to, **it clarifies**.

Creating your Mission Statement

Those with a mission have a message. Do not allow your mission to pass by – do not miss your mission! Consequently, write a mission statement that is clear and motivating to you. Even if you are unaware of your life purpose, having a mission statement will at least help you realize your vision and achieve your goals.

- **Start with Intuition**: Write down your mission as it naturally comes to you, using present tense and active language. Your authentic voice will make the statement more meaningful and memorable.
- **Be clear**: Keep it concise, specific, and explicit so that it is memorable. Avoid vague language. A well-defined mission statement helps you avoid distractions and maintain focus on your primary objectives.
- **Refine your Words**: Don't rush. Revising and refining your statement over time will make it more effective. Aim for simplicity so it's easy to remember and internalize.

- **Make it inspiring**: Your mission statement should energize and motivate you. Let it reflect your higher aspirations and serve as a source of momentum.
- **Visualize and revisit**: Display your mission statement where you'll see it daily. Priming and regular reflection will help reinforce your commitment and provide clarity on your progress.

In a Nutshell

Don't miss your mission! Your mission is more than just a statement – it's a guide to living purposefully and achieving your goals. It gives you direction. By creating a mission statement, you build a powerful tool to focus your energy and align your actions with your vision. Make it meaningful, keep it visible, and let it inspire you every day.

Reflective Questions

1. How do you want to achieve your vision and fulfill your purpose?
2. Have you composed an attractive mission statement for yourself?
3. What makes your mission unique?
4. What differentiates your mission from others with similar goals?
5. How can you stay true to your unique strengths and passions?
6. Have you implemented time to reflect? Have you implemented reflection practices of your mission statement?

Wake-up Prompts

1. One action you could take today to demonstrate excellence in fulfilling your destiny → »One bold action I take today is…«

2. »The purpose of my mission is to [*insert purpose*] by [*insert actions or methods*].«

3. »I am committed to [*insert values or priorities*] as I pursue [*insert goal*].«

4. »Through my mission, I aim to [*insert impact or outcome*] by [*insert how you'll achieve it*].«

5. »Every day, I strive to [*insert key action or behavior*] to fulfill my vision of [*insert vision or purpose*].«

6. »My mission is to live a life aligned with [*insert values or principles*] while achieving [*insert goal*].«

7. »I want to inspire and contribute to [insert audience or group] by [*insert action or purpose*].«

8. »In pursuit of my vision, I will [*insert actions*] to overcome [*insert challenges*] and achieve [*insert results*].«

9. »My mission is to serve as a bridge between [*two ideas, groups, or goals*], ensuring [*specific outcomes*].«

10. »With focus on [*core value or purpose*], I will [*specific actions*] to bring about [*desired impact*].«

RESPONSIBILITY — Owning your Power to create

rɪˌspɒn.səˈbɪl.ɪ.ti

⠗⠊⠎⠏⠕⠝⠎⠊⠃⠊⠇⠊⠞⠽

[the quality or state of being responsible: such as a moral, legal, or mental accountability]

> With great power comes great responsibility.
> – *Stan Lee*

Responsibility (to respond, responsible) – the state of being accountable for my own actions and decisions. It involves accepting the consequences of our choices and taking full ownership of them. This fundamental trait is essential for both personal and professional growth, fostering accountability and reliability.

Responsibility, responding with responsibility, builds trust and respect. When we demonstrate responsible behavior, we not only earn others' confidence but also develop greater self-awareness and self-assurance. The moment we say, »*I am responsible, I am accountable, I have to face up to this,*« is the day we grow up. And it is the moment we are free, or at least freer than before.

A practical way to grasp the concept of responsibility is through karma – every action creates a reaction. Everything has a consequence. Our actions have a direct impact that extends beyond what we can see, requiring us to act with intention. What you do to others reflects back on you. This perspective on interconnection reminds us that how we treat others affects our own experience of life.

How can you ensure you are taking Responsibility effectively?

The key lies in honest and transparent communication. This includes acknowledging mistakes promptly and accepting their consequences. It also means being receptive to feedback and willing to make necessary adjustments.

True responsibility requires a commitment to continuous improvement. This involves reflecting on experiences, identifying areas for growth, and taking proactive steps to prevent future issues. It also means addressing challenges directly rather than avoiding them.

Taking responsibility is a testament to your character and integrity. It demonstrates a commitment to doing what's right, even when faced with difficulties. Through responsible actions, we show ourselves to be trustworthy and dependable individuals who can be counted on to fulfill our obligations.

The Language of Responsibility

The way we speak about responsibility reveals much about how we view accountability and ownership in our lives. When someone says *I will* instead of *I'll try*, they demonstrate commitment rather than hesitation. Listen to a mother, and she will teach you what commitment really means! Similarly, choosing *I made a mistake* over *mistakes were made* shows direct ownership rather than deflection.

Active voice in responsibility-focused language empowers the speaker. Compare *the deadline was missed* to *I missed the deadline* – the latter acknowledges personal agency and ownership. Words like **accountable, commit,** and **ensure** carry weight and intention, while phrases like *sort of, maybe*, and *hopefully* can dilute responsibility.

Perhaps most telling is the shift **from *but* to *and*** in accepting responsibility. Instead of saying, *I understand your concern, but...* which often precedes an excuse, saying, *I understand your concern, and here's what I'm doing about it* demonstrates both acknowledgment and action. This subtle linguistic choice transforms defensive responses into constructive dialogue.

The language we choose either reinforces or diminishes our sense of responsibility. By selecting words that embrace rather than evade accountability, we not only communicate more effectively but also cultivate a deeper sense of personal agency and trustworthiness.

In a Nutshell

When you take full responsibility, you **own your actions and their outcomes**. By communicating honestly, learning from your experiences, and actively addressing challenges, you build trust with others and strengthen your integrity. Your choice of words matters too – when you use direct, active language like *I will* instead of vague phrases like *maybe*, you demonstrate real commitment. This approach to responsibility helps you grow while earning others' respect and confidence.

Reflective Questions

1. What does responsibility mean to you?
2. For which actions do you take full responsibility in your life?
3. Where do you think you lack full responsibility?
4. When was it hardest for you to admit a mistake, and what did you learn?
5. What role does forgiveness play in responsibility?
6. If you could change some of your actions now, which choices would you revisit?

Wake-up Prompts

1. Reflect upon your actions for the next few days. Write down all responsibilities for which you take full ownership.
2. Think of a difficult situation in the past. What is the best way you would deal with it responsibly?
3. Describe a time when taking full responsibility led to unexpected positive outcomes...
4. Explore how your language changes when fully accepting versus deflecting responsibility...
5. Consider a current situation where you could take more responsibility – what specific actions could you take?
6. »I know I'm truly being responsible when...«
7. »My definition of responsibility has changed because...«
8. »The relationship between **responsibility** and **trust** is...«

Part VI: Navigating Life's Rhythms

PEACE — Cultivating inner Harmony

piːs
ˈpiː.ˈˈˈ.

[from the Anglo-French *pes*, and the Old French *pais*, meaning peace, reconciliation, silence, agreement]

> When the power of love overcomes the love of power, the world will know peace.
> – *Jimi Hendrix*

P eace (pacify, peaceful, or peaceable), with its immense depth, calls to the heart of every human Being. It is our shared quiet Hope, our collective dream of a world where fear gives way to love. Across every culture and belief system, peace stands tall as a beacon of harmony – **a sanctuary where humanity's finest qualities shine through**. But wishing alone won't bring it to life; we must learn to speak peace's language – one woven from empathy, respect, and unwavering compassion.

The Dimension of Peace

Peace is both our shelter and our journey – an embrace that soothes our Souls and a light guiding us through dark times. External peace – when violence and strife fall away – creates the foundation for justice, stability, and progress. Internal peace is our inner sanctuary, the calm that steadies our hearts when life's storms rage. The language of peace bridges these worlds, a melody that brings harmony to our inner and outer lives, creating an understanding of where division once lived.

Speaking the Language of Peace

Peace speaks not just through words but through gentle, everyday actions. It's the hand we extend in forgiveness, the patient ear we offer in understanding, and the heart we open to kindness. It lives in choosing dialogue over judgment, patience over anger, and Hope over despair. When we embrace this language, we create more than conflict resolution – we spark a chain reaction of goodwill that touches countless lives.

Peace is what our Souls genuinely yearn for, a gift we give ourselves and our world. Its power lies in healing, uniting, and inspiring. As we learn and speak peace's language, we plant seeds for a brighter tomorrow, where every heart finds rest, every voice rings clear, and every person thrives. Peace is the **melody binding us together**, a song worthy of passing down through generations.

Finding Peace in Silence

Silence has become a rare treasure. Yet, it is in silence that we often find guiding insights. It holds a healing power, connects us with the eternal. It leads us into the depths – sometimes unknown depths – to our innermost being, our heart. Through the path of the heart, we experience the Source of peace and love.

Peace and Love belong together

Peace and love are two halves of something beautiful and whole. Peace brings people together by helping us understand each other, while love connects us through deep caring. Both have this amazing ability to heal old wounds, to bring light into those dark corners of life, to show us the incredible beauty we all share as human Beings.

Neither one happens by accident, though. Peace asks us to make that choice, sometimes the hard choice, to forgive, to really listen, and to work towards harmony. Love asks the same of us in its own way – to care deeply, to nurture others, and to give without keeping score. They grow strongest in those little moments of kindness, when we put others first, and when we're brave enough to let our guards down.

They speak to everyone, everywhere. It doesn't matter what language you speak or where you're from – a warm smile, a gentle touch, a kind word carries their message straight to the heart. They break down walls between people and remind us that real strength isn't about fighting but connecting. It's not about fear but understanding each other.

They are inseparable. Every time we make peace, love is there. Every time we show love, peace follows. Together, they teach us something profound – that the sweetest victories aren't about winning over others but coming together. They're the foundation of a life that truly means something.

Peace in different Languages

Afrikaans: *verde* – Albanais: *paqe* – German: *Frieden* – Alsacian: *fréda* – Arabien: *salam* – Bulgarian: *mir* – Catalanian: *pau* – Corse: *pace* – Croatian: *u miru* – Spanish: *paz* – Espéranto: *paco* – Finnish: *rauha* – Greek: *Irini* – Hebrew : *chalom* – Hindi : *shanti* – Hungarian: *béke* – Italian: *pace* – Lituanian: *taika* – Luxemburgish : *fridden* – Dutch: *vrede* – Norvegian: *fred* – Polish: *pokoj* – Thai: *santiphaap* – Turkish: *baris*

In a Nutshell – Why Peace matters

Peace is the ultimate form of freedom. It is the fertile soil for humanity's dreams. Under its warmth, education flourishes, and societies dare to innovate. It creates a quiet stage where silenced voices finally speak, and equality finds true meaning. Without peace, hearts shatter, dreams fade – the cycle of pain continues. With peace, impossible things become possible – love overcomes fear, and our world begins to heal and unite.

Reflective Questions

1. What does peace mean to you?
2. When do you feel peaceful?
3. How do you value peace? How important is peace in your life?
4. What does the phrase »language of peace« mean to you, and how can it be practiced in everyday life?
5. How does internal peace contribute to achieving external peace in a society?
6. Why is peace considered essential for human growth and development?
7. What role does **empathy** play in resolving conflicts and fostering peace?
8. How can individuals contribute to global peace through small, personal actions?
9. What are the most significant barriers to peace in today's world, and how can they be overcome?
10. How does the absence of peace affect education, economic stability, and equality?
11. In what ways can art, culture, or literature become a medium for promoting the language of peace?
12. What is the relationship between **forgiveness** and **peace**? Can one exist without the other?
13. How do you think teaching peace and conflict resolution in schools could shape future generations?nflict resolution in schools could shape future generations?

Prompts for Peace

1. Describe a moment when you felt a profound sense of peace. How did it impact your perspective on life?
2. Imagine a world where the language of peace is the norm. What would that world look like?
3. Write a story where two conflicting communities learn to communicate using the language of peace.

4. Create a manifesto titled »The Path to Peace« outlining steps individuals and societies can take to foster harmony.
5. Reflect on a personal conflict you resolved peacefully. What language or actions helped achieve that resolution?
6. Compose a poem that captures the essence of internal and external peace.
7. Discuss the importance of empathy in bridging cultural or ideological divides in pursuit of peace.
8. Imagine you are part of a global council dedicated to peacebuilding. What strategies would you propose?
9. Write an open letter to future generations about the significance of preserving peace.
10. Explore how forgiveness can transform a relationship or situation of conflict into one of harmony.

PATIENCE — The Art of timely Waiting
'peɪ.ʃəns
⠏⠀⠀⠎⠀⠞⠀⠎⠀⠉⠑

[Patience originates from the Latin word *patientia*, which means »endurance« or »suffering,« derived from the verb *patī*, which means »to suffer« or »to endure«]

> Patience is bitter, but its fruit is sweet.
> – *Jean-Jacques Rousseau*

P atience (to be patient, patient) – both a silent virtue, a quiet strength, and an essential skill. Those who cultivate patience understand that **meaningful growth takes time**. As the saying goes, good things come to those who wait. This quality of patiently waiting enables us to weather life's inevitable delays and setbacks with grace and gratitude while maintaining our focus on long-term goals.

Patience isn't merely passive waiting but an active practice of self-regulation and wisdom. Some things cannot be rushed: the healing of a wound – as the German saying goes: *Zeit heilt alle Wunden* – the development of a relationship, or the mastery of a craft. This understanding helps us resist the modern impulse for instant gratification and allows us to make more meaningful decisions.

When we choose patience, our daily experiences transform. Traffic jams become opportunities for reflection, long lines become chances to practice mindfulness, and setbacks become lessons in resilience. In embracing patience, we don't just endure time – we learn to use it wisely, finding peace in the present moment while working steadily toward our aspirations.

If I've learned anything in life, it's that dreams become reality when I stay focused and give myself time. The path may twist and turn, and the outcome might look different from what you first imagined, but persistence and patience have a way of bringing you where you need to be. »When« is written in the stars. But it will come true – we just have to keep our hearts open and stay true to our dreams and goals.

From secondary school onward, I often felt like the slowest learner in the room – someone who couldn't grasp concepts that others seemed to understand easily. This feeling followed me from school into my professional life, where I constantly believed I was eons behind my peers. This was the case for practically all areas of my life (except for Sports and geography). Years, sometimes decades later, I experienced a profound shift in perspective. Everything clicked into place as connections formed between previously disconnected ideas. What once seemed like a permanent limitation had transformed into clarity and understanding. I could finally connect the dots – Patience was harvested.

Patience is a valuable Value

Patience is more than a personal trait. It is a profound value that shapes human behavior and relationships. As a value, it reflects qualities such as respect, self-control, and trust in the natural flow of life. In a world driven by speed and immediate results, patience stands as a counterbalance, promoting mindfulness and deeper connections.

At its core, patience embodies respect for others, for oneself, and the process of growth. It allows individuals to navigate challenges with grace, offering the necessary time and space for understanding and healing. Patience fosters self-discipline, teaching us to control impulses and endure temporary discomfort for greater rewards.

Patience strengthens relationships by encouraging empathy and tolerance. When we exercise patience, we listen more deeply and judge less hastily, building trust and mutual respect. It is through patience that we find the ability to mend misunderstandings and sustain long-term bonds.

Ultimately, patience as a value enriches both personal and communal life. It reminds us that enduring moments of uncertainty with calm and resilience can lead to profound growth and fulfillment. By embracing patience, we cultivate a more compassionate and harmonious world.

The Language of Patience

The language of patience is unspoken yet profound. It is conveyed through calm actions, thoughtful decisions, and measured responses. This language transcends words, as it is often demonstrated through the way one handles adversity. When faced with obstacles, the patient communicates trust in the process and faith in eventual outcomes. Their demeanor exudes a quiet assurance that things will unfold as they are meant to, fostering a sense of calm not only within themselves but also in those around them.

Patience teaches us to **listen deeply and observe carefully**. It encourages us to pause before reacting, to understand rather than to judge, and to empathize rather than to dismiss. This silent language fosters stronger relationships, as it builds trust and mutual respect. In essence, patience speaks to the heart, reminding us that time and understanding are powerful tools for connection.

Patience as the Mirror of Perseverance

Patience and perseverance are often viewed as complementary virtues. While both are rooted in resilience and the ability to endure, their approaches to adversity and challenges differ in tone and action. Patience is the quiet strength that allows us **to endure calmly**, while perseverance is the active pursuit of a goal, overcoming obstacles with determination and effort.

Patience, as the passive mirror image of perseverance, reflects an inner stillness and acceptance. It requires the wisdom to know when to pause and let time take its course. In contrast, perseverance demands energy and action, a refusal to give up despite setbacks. Together, they form a harmonious balance: patience ensures we do not act rashly or out of frustration, while perseverance drives us to keep moving forward, ensuring progress.

This interplay is essential for success. For example, a farmer must patiently wait for crops to grow after planting seeds, but the act of tending the soil and watering the plants is perseverance in action. Similarly, patience fosters understanding and healing in relationships, while perseverance helps build and sustain bonds through continuous effort.

In a Nutshell

Patience is both a silent virtue and an active skill that fosters grace, self-regulation, and wisdom. It teaches us to endure delays, setbacks, and challenges with calmness, emphasizing the importance of time for growth, healing, and meaningful connections. As a profound value, patience reflects respect, self-control, and trust, enhancing relationships and promoting mindfulness in a fast-paced world. It complements perseverance by balancing stillness with action, creating a harmonious interplay essential for success and resilience. Together, patience and perseverance enrich personal and communal life, guiding us toward fulfillment and a more compassionate existence.

Reflective Questions

1. In which areas of your life do you think you are patient? In which areas do you think you are less patient?
2. Do you think patience is undervalued in today's fast-paced society? Why or why not?
3. What practices help you to resist the impulse for instant gratification?
4. What do you think – does time reveal everything?
5. How can you become more patient?

Wake-up Prompts for Patience

1. Think of a situation where patience helped you heal emotionally. How did the outcome of that situation change?
2. Write a journal entry from the perspective of »Patience« personified. What does it feel, see, or want to say?
3. How do the qualities of patience differ from the qualities of perseverance, and where do they overlap?

PERSEVERANCE — Staying the Course

ˌpɜː.sɪˈvɪə.rəns

[persistence in doing something despite difficulty or delay in achieving success]

> Great works are performed not by strength, but perseverance.
> – *Samuel Johnson*

Perseverance (persevere, persistent) – that **deep inner drive that keeps us going** when things get tough. Think of it as the bridge between our dreams and reality, the conscious choice to turn our goals into actual results. It's not just about hanging on; it's about actively moving forward. To stay committed in the face of challenging circumstances.

Perseverance and patience are close relatives. However, there are subtle differences. You might say patience is perseverance's quieter cousin – it's more about inner strength and staying power than actively pushing forward. Perseverance helps build both consistency and patience, but it's got that extra spark of **active determination**. Especially when times are tough, perseverance helps to stay afloat and tide us over temporary setbacks.

Perseverance is often associated with strong discipline. It contains a particular calling to achieve something. It takes tenacity to achieve one's personal worthwhile goals, and any worthwhile goal is challenging and seems to involve some suffering. Otherwise, it just doesn't seem worthwhile or valuable. Perseverance is often associated with hardship, yet it is one of the most beautiful things life has to offer. This is often realized in retrospect. The most beautiful memories and feelings stem from personal adventures in which we gave our all and overcame obstacles. These positive feelings touch our deeper level of emotions and are what make memories truly unforgettable. The intensity of a positive emotion directly correlates with the strength of the corresponding memory.

But we shouldn't persevere at all costs. Sometimes quitting is the better solution and makes you more fulfilled than persisting in an activity that brings you less fulfillment.

Waiting is hard

Especially in today's fast-paced world, perseverance is a crucial value to possess. With everything moving at lightning speed, we often feel a nagging fear of missing out – FOMO. This is detrimental to what we strive for in life, which can take years to pay off. Waiting for extended periods goes against our human nature, as it means sacrificing immediate gratification for a postponed but ultimately more fulfilling, higher outcome. We at least hope for this to happen.

I've come to realize that resistance is a necessity for growth, like a runner who needs the friction of the ground or a swimmer who needs the pressure of the water. You don't go against it, but with it. You learn to dance effortlessly with this omnipresent force. Effortless because of it. I've felt how challenges shape me, forcing me forward even when it's tough. Without struggle, there's no real strength, no transformation.

Why should we still wait for the delayed Reward?

The feeling of satisfaction after accomplishing something meaningful is indescribable. You feel spent and satisfied at the same time. Whether it's for the benefit of loved ones, the environment, or oneself, doing something meaningful gives life depth. Pursuing something that aligns with one's values is meaningful and fulfilling.

Achieving perseverance becomes easier when you have a passion for what you do and persist until the end. Even though persevering through something that doesn't ignite your passion can be valuable, it is undeniably simpler to achieve a long-term goal when you love what you do and feel energized by it.

We are all **Sisyphus** in some way. But if we choose our struggle, embrace it, and make peace with its endlessness, we transform from prisoners of fate into masters of perseverance. Not because we will reach the top, but because we refuse to stop climbing.

With time and dedication, your efforts will yield remarkable results. Investing in something worthwhile pays off in the end, and you'll be astonished at how much you've accomplished. One day, hopefully, you will look back, and as you reflect on your past experiences, you may be amazed and appreciative of how much you have achieved. As the German saying goes, *Geduld bringt Rosen* – literally, patience brings roses. Stay patient, keep going, keep growing, and let perseverance light your way.

When I hear Perseverance, I think of...

Tenacity – grit – stamina – unwavering determination – volition – commitment – willpower – assiduousness – a truly resolved person – the conscious, deliberate conversion of motives and goals into results – an implementation skill – faith in the process – a quiet but active strength – a defiant optimism – lived patience – patience in action – the art of enduring – I almost can't bear it any longer, but somehow I got through

In a Nutshell

Perseverance is that essential inner drive that turns goals into reality. While related to patience and consistency, it's more active, pushing us forward when things get tough. In today's world of instant gratification, perseverance becomes even more valuable because meaningful achievements take time. Though challenging, the satisfaction of persevering toward worthwhile goals creates our most cherished memories and deeply fulfills us, especially when we're passionate about what we're pursuing.

Never give up, my friend. The person you are becoming needs you!

Reflective Questions

1. Where have you shown the ability to persist? Can you mention a specific example?
2. When have you shown the greatest perseverance in your life? What drove you to keep going?
3. In which areas do you feel you are particularly persistent?
4. Where do you lose patience relatively quickly, and are you more impatient? Are there possibilities for more patience in these areas as well?
5. When you look back on your life, where and how has your persistence paid off?
6. Are you consistent and persistent in the areas you consider important? How can you become more persistent and patient in these areas?
7. Are there areas in your life where you wish you had shown more perseverance? What stopped you?
8. Do you think perseverance is an innate quality, or can it be developed over time? Why?
9. What motivates humans to persevere in the face of adversity? Is it hope, pride, survival, or something else?
10. How does perseverance shape our identity and self-worth?

Wake-up Prompts for Perseverance

1. Try to remember your goals. Set your daily focus on them. This is a priming measure.
2. Set your plan/calendar in alignment with your goals.
3. Try to lower disturbances as much as possible. Don't allow push notifications to interrupt your work.
4. If it's not already done, clean your sleeping room from disturbers like your mobile phone or television.
5. Set daily habits to achieve your goals. You don't need to execute daily but on a constant rhythm (little by little becomes a lot).
6. Remember: High-priority actions instead of low-priority distractions.
7. Write a short story about a character whose perseverance changes their life or the lives of others.
8. »Perseverance is like ___ because ___.«
9. Think of someone who embodies perseverance. What qualities do they possess that inspire you?
10. How do small, consistent actions contribute to perseverance in the long term? Reflect on a goal where this has been true for you.
11. *Everything that is accomplished fast vanishes fast.* Would you agree with this statement?

FREEDOM — Breaking through Limitations
ˈfriː.dəm

⠋⠗⠊⠙⠕⠍

[**a:** the power or right to act, speak, or think as one wants; **b:** the state of not being imprisoned or enslaved]

> For to be free is not merely to cast off one's chains,
> but to live in a way that respects and enhances the freedom
> of others.
> – *Nelson Mandela*

Freedom (to free, to be free) – how this word stirs something deep within us! Whether it's the power to act as our heart's desire or the profound state of being unbound by chains, freedom weaves two beautiful threads into the tapestry of human experience. Ask ten human Souls about freedom, and you'll hear ten different stories, each colored by their own journey through life.

Freedom is the extraordinary gift to choose in every moment of our lives. Even in our darkest times, we hold the power to choose how we think and feel. This **inner sanctuary of thought** remains ours alone – a flame that outside forces cannot extinguish. Our thoughts are one treasure that can never truly be taken from us.

When do we truly feel free?

Sometimes, we create our own prison in our minds. Addictive behaviors create stress that weighs us down, trapping us in destructive thought patterns and self-imposed limitations more restrictive than physical barriers. In such situations, I often close my eyes and remember powerful moments. Those transcendent moments: standing breathless on a mountain peak, the world sprawled endlessly before me, or watching a bird soar through boundless skies, crossing invisible borders as if they were nothing but whispers in the wind. Freedom floods our Beings when we stand alone with our choices, when no voices but our own inner wisdom guide our path.

Why do we yearn so deeply for Freedom?

One reason might be our desire for more autonomy and self-determination. Freedom is the soil in which our dreams take root. When we're free, our Spirits can stretch toward whatever star calls to us, unlimited by the shadows of doubt or constraint. It's in this spacious possibility that we find our truest purpose, our deepest calling.

Another reason many of us seek freedom lies in the relaxing response of our bodies when we feel free. There's something magical that happens in our bodies when freedom takes hold – have you felt it? The way our chest expands, as if our hearts could touch the horizon. How our breath flows freely like a river finding its way to the sea, carrying life-giving energy to every cell. In these moments, feelings of fear and doubt dissolve like morning mist, leaving us standing in **the clear light of limitless potential.**

What is the Value of Freedom?

The value of freedom shifts like light through a prism, taking on different colors depending on where we stand. For those living under the heavy hand of oppression, freedom might feel like water in the desert. For others blessed with an abundance of choice, it might feel as natural as breathing. Yet there's one freedom that belongs to us all – the sovereignty of our inner world. Viktor E. Frankl, who survived the concentration camp, the harshest circumstances imaginable, aptly described this in the following words: *Between stimulus and response there is a space. In that space is our power to choose our response. In our response lies our growth and our freedom.* No matter what walls surround us, our thoughts and feelings remain our own, a garden we tend in the privacy of our hearts.

How can you cultivate Freedom in your own Life?

By giving ourselves permission to be vast and unlimited, we can nurture freedom in the soil of our own lives. Look closely at what holds you back – are they real chains, or shadows of doubt we can step through? Remember, like water, freedom finds many paths to flow. Free yourself from doubts. Let attachment to the past go. Let your chest expand with each breath, feel your heart space open like wings catching the wind. Let your body remember what it means to be boundless.

In a Nutshell

Freedom is the power to think, feel, and act without restraint. It's standing on a mountaintop, feeling the wind, or chasing dreams with nothing holding you back. Freedom lets you breathe deeply, filling your heart with possibility and your mind with clarity. It's not just a right – it's a feeling, a state of being limitless, where the weight of fear and doubt melts away, leaving only boundless potential. Most precious of all, it's the quiet knowing that within you lives an **unconquerable space where your Spirit roams free**, where possibility blooms eternal.

How does freedom sing in your heart?

Reflective Questions

1. What does freedom mean to you personally?
2. When was the last time you truly felt free? What made you feel that way?
3. Do you think freedom is more about external circumstances or internal mindset? Why?
4. How does your environment or culture shape your perception of freedom?
5. Can true freedom ever exist, or is it always limited in some way?
6. What do you think: When you take full responsibility for your actions, does this give you less or more freedom? Why?
7. What do political rights mean to you in the context of freedom, such as freedom of expression or freedom of religion?

Wake-up Prompts for Freedom

1. Dance yourself free! Describe a moment in your life when you felt completely free. What emotions and sensations accompanied that experience?
2. Write about a time when you felt restricted or confined. How did you navigate that situation, and what did it teach you about freedom?
3. Imagine you could change one rule or limitation in your life to feel freer. What would it be, and why?
4. Explore the idea of freedom as a state of mind. How can someone cultivate freedom regardless of external circumstances?
5. Reflect on the connection between freedom and responsibility. Can we have one without the other?

FAITH — The unwavering Light
feɪθ
∷ ˙ ∴ ⣀ ⣀

[*fidere* in Latin, »to trust«]

Faith is the strength
by which a shattered world shall
emerge into the light.
– *Helen Keller*

F AITH (having faith, being faithful) is the free breathing of
the Soul. The feeling when you take a deep breath – suddenly
everything feels possible. It's that quiet strength inside us that
makes us brave enough to take the next step, even when we can't
see the whole path ahead.

Mark Nepo once described faith beautifully as *our covenant
with life*. In this sense, think of faith as your anchor. It's that gut
feeling, that deep trust, in German called *Urvertrauen* – the kind
of primal trust you had as a child when you believed anything
was possible.

For me personally, faith is so important because it not only
gives me energy and power in good times, but, most importantly,
in sad times as well. It's like an elixir of and for life. Faith and a
patient attitude are two of these healing, strengthening energies
that keep you going even in the darkest of times. Believe me, the
aha-moments are waiting on the other side.

Faith – its Roots and its Imagination

Faith and confidence (*confidential* in Latin, derived from *con-fido*,
meaning »with trust«) are closely intertwined and share a common root in trust; they are inseparable. Trust is the fertile ground
in which faith grows. Without trust, it becomes challenging to
maintain a faithful attitude. At the same time, trust is nurtured by
a faithful attitude. Faith can be described as the profound belief
we hold within ourselves. Our Hope with a capital H.

Faith fuels the imagination, allowing us to **see beyond present**

limitations. It's the writer who writes a story without knowing how it will end or the entrepreneur who risks everything on an idea because they believe in its potential.

The Language of Faith

When you're searching for faith's voice, you'll find it in the most unexpected places. The friend who calls just when you need them most, the sunrise that promises a new beginning, the gentle sound of waves that reminds you of life's constant rhythm. Sometimes, it's just a whisper in your heart, telling you to hold on just a little longer.

I've always felt that faith speaks in its own beautiful way – it's a language that doesn't rely on words but is understood deep in the heart and Soul. It's that quiet, reassuring voice that lifts you up when the world feels heavy and uncertain. It's the gentle whisper of Hope that flows through every part of you, **shining through the shadows of doubt**. You feel it in your bones when you witness an act of kindness, or when you stand beneath a star-filled sky. It's in the quiet moments of prayer, in the warmth of a loving embrace, in the courage to start over.

The language of faith is gentle yet powerful. It speaks through symbols, through rituals, through moments of stillness and prayer. It speaks through the confidence you show in your actions and the love you share. It opens a dialogue with yourself, the world, and the unknown.

Faith is also the language of connection. It links you to your innermost Self and to all that is greater than you. It reminds you that you are never alone and that there is always a reason to continue to Hope and to believe in the impossible. Sometimes, faith speaks through another person – a friend's encouraging word or an act of kindness. Often, it speaks through nature – the blooming flower, the rising moon, the rushing sea.

Among the many inner voices that try to convince us, the traffic within, one stands out as the guiding force. **The voice** that brings harmony, **that rises from the depths of your Soul**. When you begin to trust and follow this voice, faith begins to blossom. Following your heartfelt voice is a commitment; through this commitment, faith strengthens.

How Faith and Courage dance together

Faith and courage go hand in hand in everything we do. Faith is believing in something even when we can't see the outcome, and courage is taking action despite fear or uncertainty. Even seeking happiness requires both – faith that we deserve it and courage to pursue it, even, especially, when obstacles stand in our way.

Faith is the driving force behind courage. As the French word *coeur* suggests, courage is born from the heart, infused with the energy of faith. Boldness – the fearless leap – is powered by this energy, carrying genius and transformative strength within it.

But courage also plays a significant role in strengthening faith. When we take brave steps, we often find a renewed trust in ourselves and our path, which in turn deepens our faith. Both courage and faith are crucial when facing life's uncertainties: Faith provides Hope and direction, while courage empowers us to push through challenges.

As faith deepens, self-awareness tends to flourish as well. Through humility and mindfulness, faith fosters gentleness, a quiet strength that steadies us. Germans call it *Sanftmut*, gentle courage.

Faith as an Amplifier

Have you ever noticed how faith makes everything feel bigger, brighter? Faith has the unique power to amplify everything it touches. It takes a quiet Hope and turns it into a roaring belief. Faith has a unique way of transforming our small, hesitant steps into powerful strides filled with purpose and conviction. It doesn't just add to what we already have; instead, it acts like a multiplier, enhancing our inner strengths and broadening the possibilities that surround us.

When doubt begins to undermine our resolve, faith steps in to uplift our courage. If fear shrouds our vision, faith shines a light on what's possible, guiding us forward. It empowers us to persevere, to love unconditionally, and to dream beyond what seems achievable. The ordinary actions we take become extraordinary expressions of trust and hope.

What's more, as we let our inner light shine through faith, it becomes contagious. It inspires those around us, creating a ripple effect of positivity and strength. It reminds us that belief is a powerful force that grows stronger each time we share it with others.

Acting on faith brings clarity and is a door opener for commitment. For commitment to materialize, faith is essential. The stronger your faith, the more trust you have in your choices and actions. It encourages action and transforms ideas into reality.

The living Firmament of Faith

The foundation of faith lies in healthy questioning, which keeps it dynamic and alive, as Helen Keller observed. A Spirit of optimism and a curious environment further sustain and re-invigorate faith. Having faith and trust in something greater – a higher power – cultivates gratitude and infuses life with meaning.

The firmament of faith feels like this vibrant, living space that surrounds and uplifts us. It's not something fixed or limited; it's constantly growing, evolving, and adapting to the unique rhythms of our lives. Just like the sky above us, this expanse of faith stretches endlessly, reminding us both of our small role in the universe and our profound importance within it.

This living firmament thrives on our beliefs and is nourished by our experiences. Each time we trust or show courage, it's as if we're adding another star to this vast sky. It flourishes in an environment filled with hope and an open heart, where asking questions and being curious are seen as opportunities to deepen our understanding rather than as something frightening. Faith invites us to explore its mysteries and to find solace in its steadfastness.

Hope shines brightly within this firmament, illuminating our dreams and the possibilities we yearn for. Whenever doubt creeps in and dims our perspective, this expanse remains – a gentle reminder that faith persists, even through the darkest times. It softly encourages us: »Look up. Trust. You're not alone.«

What's truly beautiful about this firmament is how it connects us to one another. As Mark Nepo beautifully put it, *When faithful*

– when full of faith – we reveal the force that joins us. Faith creates a shared sky that we all walk under, no matter where we come from or where we're headed. It fosters empathy and unity, reminding us that while we may follow different paths, we're all guided by the same constellations of Hope and trust.

To live within this firmament is to fully embrace life's joys and challenges, certainties and mysteries. It is to know that the ground beneath your feet and the sky above your head are held together by the boundless energy of faith.

> Faith teaches us to use our talents to the fullest extent, however slight they may be. Even if a frail body refuses to obey the Soul's big behests, one can always do the little nameless things that give life grace and meaning. Simple goodness is 'the dear essential of the heart,' and the universe of the little significant lives is as vast as the universe of the stars.
> *– Helen Keller*

In a Nutshell

Faith is **what keeps you going** when everything feels uncertain – the Spirit of encouragement. It's that quiet voice that says, **try again**, when you want to give up. It's trust in what you can't yet see and Hope for what's still out of reach. Faith gives your dreams wings and strengthens your heart for the journey. It doesn't erase the struggle, but it makes it bearable, transforming doubts into possibilities and fears into courage. Faith reminds you that you are not alone and that something beautiful is waiting on the other side of belief. So, my friend, I dearly encourage you to take the leap of faith!

I opened and I will close with the words of Helene Keller:
Faith is a brave look of the Soul for new paths to life.

Reflective Questions

1. What is the significance of faith to you?
2. How would you describe your faith journey? How does faith guide you in your daily life? What role does faith play in your daily decisions?
3. How do you nurture trust within yourself and others?
4. In what ways can healthy questioning strengthen your faith?
5. In what ways do you cultivate trust within yourself and others?
6. When do you feel the presence of God, the Universe? How does it feel like?
7. Do you trust in the basic goodness of the universe?
8. Do you think taking the initiative and having a clear intention fuels confidence?
9. Do you think you have uphill hopes but downhill habits? How can you initiate better habits?

Wake-up Prompts for Faith

1. Write a letter to your future self, sharing your current Hopes and dreams, and trust that faith will guide you towards them.
2. Faith is a language we learn by living it: Spend a moment in silence, visualizing the realization of a deeply held dream. Let faith strengthen your resolve.
3. Recall a time when you acted courageously because of faith. Reflect on how that moment shaped you.
4. Take a small, bold step toward something you've been hesitant to pursue, trusting that faith will carry you.
5. When *what-if* questions pop up, try to formulate them in a positive way. For example, instead of thinking, *what if I'm failing?* think of *what if I'm succeeding?* Remember, words and questions have power! \
6. Now, move forward, face the sunrise, and embrace life's challenges with unwavering trust.

Part VII: The Integrated Life

HEALTH — Nurturing your whole Being
hɛlθ
∴ ∵ ˙ ⋮ ⦂∴

[**wholeness**, a state of being and feeling whole, sound, or well]

> The greatest wealth is health.
> – *Virgil*

Health (being healthy, healthy) is emphasized the most in its holistic significance – human Beings are holistic systems. We thrive when we achieve balance, when our **yin and yang are in alignment**, across all dimensions: physical, mental, emotional, and spiritual. When we're healthy, we feel complete, whole. *Mens sana in corpore sana* – every physical exercise is essential to mental and psychological well-being. That's maybe why health, wholeness, and holiness share ancient linguistic roots. They all trace back to the Proto-Germanic word *hailitho-* or *hailaz*, meaning »whole,« »uninjured,« or »complete.«

Health forms the foundation for everything else we want to experience, especially well-being. Taking care of ourselves requires intentional choices – nourishing food, regular movement, and nurturing our mental health. This investment in ourselves not only opens the door to a more joyful life but also inspires us to live our best life. That's why health isn't just about avoiding illness; it's about embracing wellness in its fullest sense.

Health is only perceived through personal awareness, something that often gets lost in our hectic lives. Yet, once this awareness comes to light, we will be very grateful for what we have.

The four Pillars of Health come down to one

Like everything meaningful in life, health is deeply personal, but at its core, health can be broken down into the following four pillars:

1. **Movement**: Health is movement. Life itself is in constant motion – even in sleep, we're never truly still. The key is finding our own rhythm: what types of physical activity serve us best, how often we need it, and at what intensity and variety.
2. **Rest**: We need to balance activity and rest; pushing too hard for too long takes its toll on both body and Spirit. An energy curve swings up and down, and so do we. Good sleep is when our Soul refreshes our body. Therefore, quality, consistency, and duration of your sleep are key.
3. **Nutrition**: A balanced diet, rich in vitamins and minerals, especially »the energy of the soil,« is crucial to a healthy life. Remember, healthy food is good for your mood.
4. **Well-being**: Finding and being conscious of the center of the body and resting point are part of our mental and emotional well-being, which is the prerequisite for a well-balanced life.

What we can observe and conclude is that everything needs **balance - tension and easing alternate**. Even our most enduring muscle, our heart, follows this pattern. The higher the tension, the higher the relaxation. In every moment, everything is in perfect balance. The protagonists are always counterweighted by the antagonists. Your supposed opponent is your best friend.

When does one become aware of one's Health?

When do we truly recognize the value of our health? The old saying *your health is your wealth* rings true – surveys consistently show that good health is central to a fulfilling life and tops our gratitude lists. Often, though, it takes a pivotal moment – a breath-catching instant that feels endless – to truly appreciate this gift. Sometimes, it's hearing or reading something that strikes a deep chord, suddenly opening our eyes to what we have.

The older I get, the more I understand what a gift **a sane body truly is**. It's really **the Angel of the Soul**, your only home. I speak from personal experiences of pain and suffering. Over the years, I had severe hip pain, especially during running, because of a constant suppression of my feelings. It was clearly an overload of training, striking the same structures over and over again. It manifested in my right hip and was only released after I changed my movement patterns. After experiencing many other injuries as a runner, I realized I could not outpace my pain, not run away from life. I've come to feel my body in a way I never did before – aware of every ache, every movement, every part of me. It's as if I'm finally inhabiting myself fully, appreciating what it means to be well. The lesson I learned: the older you get (bodily), the more you grow into your body and the more you feel you have to go the way of your heart, your genuine nature.

What is the deeper meaning of Health?

I sometimes wonder about the relationship between health and being truly alive. While I can't imagine life without my current physical capabilities, I know that health is a precious gift from God, the universe, one that enables us to help others and de-serves our deepest gratitude.

Health truly does heal us – and that's something to be pro-foundly thankful for.

Call for a healthy Way of doing and being

Your health is more than just feeling good physically – it's about finding balance (and romance) in all aspects of life. Take the time to move mindfully, whether it's through exercise, meditation, or simply being in tune with your daily rhythms. Remember, **a healthy person has a thousand wishes, a sick person has just one**. Health is a precious gift, and it only gets better when you take care of it. So, cherish and cultivate it – don't wait until it's too late.

Reflective Questions

1. How do you feel physically, mentally, emotionally, and spiritually?

2. What kind of health practices do you maintain?
3. How much time do you set aside for taking care of yourself and your health?
4. Have you experienced any health setbacks? If so, how did you handle it, and what was helpful during that challenging time? What did you learn from this experience?
5. Would you agree with the saying: *The body is the mirror of the Soul?* Why?
6. What personal experiences have shifted your awareness about your health? How did these moments change your perspective?
7. How do you define »movement« in your life beyond just physical exercise? What other forms of movement contribute to your overall health?
8. How has your relationship with health evolved? What wisdom have you gained through this journey?
9. What is more important to you: Your lifespan (quantity) or health span (quality)?

Wake-up Prompts for Health

1. Describe a moment when you felt profound gratitude for your health. What made this moment particularly meaningful?
2. Write about your personal »tipping point« that changed how you view or prioritize your health.
3. Explore the connection between movement and life in your experience. How does staying in motion – physically, mentally, or spiritually – affect your well-being?
4. Reflect on the balance between activity and rest in your life. How do you know when you need more of one or the other?
5. Consider the phrase *Health is God's and the Universe's blessing.* What does this mean to you personally, and how does it influence your approach to well-being?
6. *Our issues are in our tissues.* What do you think of and feel about this quote by Tara Brach?

PRESENCE — Living fully in the Now
'prɛzəns

⠏⠗⠑⠵�

[the state or fact of existing, occurring, or being present]

> When you are present, you can sense the Spirit of things,
> the beauty, the sacredness of life.
> – *Eckhardt Tolle*

P resence (to be present) – to feel the pulse of your existence, connect deeply with the world around you, and simply be fully aligned with this very moment. A kind of awakening, a realization that you are here, right now. From no-where to now-here. And really, what could be more beautiful than that?

Have you ever stopped and truly noticed the magic of this moment? Really noticed it. When what you see (in your eye) and what you think (in your mind's eye) are in alignment? In the present moment, you have **no time to rush**.

Sometimes, I catch myself wondering about the incredible paradox of being alive. Every single thing we experience is technically already in the past – even the starlight we see traveled light-years to reach us, whispering stories of celestial bodies that might not even exist anymore. Every moment is a whisper from the past. It's mind-blowing when you think about it.

Still, when we observe life, when we notice what's happening around us and within us, there's something deeply reassuring about it. You realize you belong here. You are part of this Earth, contributing to the beauty of life simply by existing. And instead of losing yourself in thoughts of the past or future, you're invited to turn inward, to look around, and to notice what brings you contentment right now. That contentment opens the door to the full range of human emotions: joy, sadness, wonder, gratitude.

The present moment, the eternal Now, though, is fleeting. This infinitesimally small piece of time. We should rather see it as »present movement.« It's an ever-changing vibrational life dance. Present-moment thinking seems rare compared to our constant schedule for the future and thinking of the past. It appears, and it disappears. It's here, and then it's gone. And there's something profoundly beautiful about that. When you let go of a moment, it's gone completely – and yet, somehow, it's still with you. Life is full of these contradictions, these little paradoxes that make it all the more meaningful.

Presence is as simple as stop, look, go. STOP, LOOK, GO. It sounds so simple yet – believe me – it proves so rare.

Presence and its close Relationships with other Qualities

Presence is like a quiet symphony that emerges when certain qualities align – attention, mindfulness, and awareness. While these concepts are interconnected, presence stands out as the deeper, more expansive experience of fully showing up for life.

Presence does not always mean focusing on the current process, but sometimes means focusing on the outcome, the future. Imagine a situation where you have strong pain, and you want to see and feel yourself in a healed state. In such cases, the focus may better shift toward the outcome than the process. Yes, face the truth, but focus on the outcome! The key is that you are aware of it and that you really pay attention to what you have intended to focus on.

I must confess that my thoughts often spin around the same topic, where I have burnt my hands or what I really want to do, or switch from one to the other like an electrical switch. As an Enneagram type 7 & 3, it is very tough not to think about the past or the future. Being fully present, in the moment, is very difficult for me.

Attention: The focusing Lens

Attention is like a spotlight that illuminates the present moment. It's precise, directional, almost mathematical in its ability to zero in on specifics. When you truly pay attention, the world comes into sharp focus – details emerge that were previously invisible. As Mary Oliver wrote in her essay Upstream, *attention is the beginning of devotion*. Nevertheless, attention alone is mechanical. It can observe without genuinely experiencing.

I would really like to emphasize this attribute. For thousands of years, we had a lack of information or were in constant search for information. In our world today, it's the complete opposite. We have information overload from all sides. We live in abundance, especially an abundance of information. That's why discernment, filtering out all we interpret as noise, is key. We have to declutter, focusing all our attention and energy on quality activities. That does not necessarily mean doing less, but doing less among what I understand to be a distraction and paying full attention to quality activities. Relaxation kicks in. This I call a balsam for the Soul.

Mindfulness: The deliberate Practice

Mindfulness is the disciplined approach to being present. Think of it as meditation in motion – a conscious, intentional way of experiencing the moment. It's like a skilled musician practicing scales, developing the muscle memory of awareness. Mindfulness teaches us to observe without judgment, to be curious about our inner landscape.

The beauty of mindfulness is its intentionality. It's a practice of gently bringing yourself back when your mind wanders, of creating space between stimulus and response. But presence transcends practice – it becomes a natural state of being.

Awareness: The expansive Consciousness

Wherever you go, there you are. – *Jon Kabat-Zinn*

No matter where we physically travel or what circumstances change around us, we bring our consciousness, our way of being, and our present-moment awareness with us.

Awareness, the vast, boundless sky in which all experiences occur. This openness and spacefulness where we feel at peace. It's not about focusing on something specific but about recognizing the entire field of experience. Awareness allows you to notice thoughts, emotions, and sensations without getting entangled in them.

Imagine sitting by a river. Attention might notice a specific ripple. Mindfulness might observe how the water moves. Awareness encompasses the entire river, the banks, the sky, the experience of sitting – all at once.

Presence: The embodied Experience

Presence is where these qualities merge into something more significant. It's not just observing life, but fully participating in it. Presence is an alive, dynamic state where you're completely engaged – body, mind, and Spirit. And whenever your attention begins to wander to the past or future, come back to your body to the here and now and focus on your breath.

The Language of Presence

The language of presence is quiet but profound. Presence speaks to us through all we perceive. It doesn't rely on words – its true power lies in how it makes you feel. It's the steady eye contact that says, »I see you.« It's the silence that holds space when no words are needed. It's the way someone listens – not just to your voice, but to what you mean, to what you feel.

This language speaks through energy, through attention, through the simple act of showing up fully. It's in a gentle touch, an understanding nod, a shared moment of stillness. The language of presence invites connection – real, deep connection – because it reminds us that we're not alone.

To speak this language is to offer yourself fully, to be here, with an open heart and a quiet mind. It's not about saying the right thing; it's about being the right thing – a calm, compassionate presence. And sometimes, that says more than words ever could.

We travel so far only to land where we are. We imagine other lives, only to meet who we are. We seek out love in special ways, only to find everyone is special. Humbly, we can't avoid this journey. It is precisely through it that, if blessed, we wake to the life we want by being present to the life we have.
– *Mark Nepo*

The Beauty of Presence

There is something truly beautiful about presence. It's like a quiet light that glows within you, bringing warmth to the Soul, or a spark from the outside that ignites your heart, reminding you that you're alive, here, connected to something greater. It can be as simple as sunlight dancing on your skin, a shared glance that says everything, or the stillness of a moment where the world seems to pause just for you. Or **the baby's smile**. Presence doesn't demand attention – **it simply is**, and in its simplicity, it has the power to transform even the most ordinary moments into something extraordinary.

Why is being present so valuable?

Being present is a quiet kind of magic. It's when you stop chasing time – no worrying about yesterday, no planning for tomorrow – and just let yourself be here. Fully. Completely. It's in this space where life feels the most real, where everything slows down just enough for you to notice how alive you are.

Presence isn't about silencing your thoughts or forcing yourself to stay still. Thoughts will wander, and that's okay. What matters is how willing you are to show up for the moment – how ready you are to let it touch your heart, fill you up, or even overwhelm you.

And it can overwhelm you. Sometimes, you'll find yourself so immersed, so belonging to this one fleeting moment, that it feels like your heart might burst. Gratitude comes rushing in, and you realize how lucky you are just to be here. And then – this is the beautiful part – you wish the same for others. You wish that every being on this Earth could feel this same lightness, this same deep joy.

But here's the tender truth: those moments don't last. The present moment comes and goes, appearing like a gift, then slipping through your fingers. And when it disappears, what's left? A soft hum of memory. A sense that, for just a moment, you were there. You were alive in the truest way.

That's why being present is so valuable. It humbles us. It reminds us of how precious and fragile life is, how beautiful it is to be human, even in the ordinary moments, even in the messy ones.

Presence connects

There's something profound that happens when we truly arrive in the present. **We** start to **feel connected** – not just to ourselves, but to everything around us. It's what lets you look someone in the eyes and really see them. It's what allows you to feel the wind on your face and remember, even for a second, how incredible it is just to exist. Suddenly, we're not just isolated individuals, but part of this incredible, interconnected web of life.

And in those moments of deep presence, something beautiful emerges: compassion. A gentle wish that everyone could experience this same sense of aliveness, this same connection.

People don't actually want your presents, they want your full presence!

How to feel more present

Accepting and embracing life as it unfolds is complex. The present is always here, but sometimes we need a little help to find our way back to it. There's no perfect formula – it's about what resonates with you, what feels like coming home. We often need habits or rituals to remind us how short-lived the present is.

I've learned that being present doesn't mean having a perfectly calm mind. Our thoughts will wander – that's just what minds do. The magic is in catching yourself, in gently bringing your attention back to this moment, again and again. It's like a beautiful dance of awareness.

Some days, presence feels like a warm embrace. Other days, it feels like standing vulnerable and raw in the middle of everything. And that's okay. Being human means experiencing the full, messy, gorgeous spectrum of emotions.

Sometimes, it's as simple as:
- **Deep Breathing**: Focusing on the breath is the most direct way to be in the here and now. It's about feeling the breath moving in and out of your lungs, hearing the subtle sounds around you, sensing the aliveness that pulses through your body.
- **Meditation**: Whether you sit, walk, or simply breathe,

meditation is like pressing pause on the noise. You don't have to do it perfectly – just show up for yourself and let the moment unfold.

- **Being in Nature**: Walk through a forest, feel the ocean breeze, or sit under a tree. Let the world remind you that you're a part of something bigger. Listen to the wind. Watch the light. Notice how alive everything feels.
- **Flow States** or **Losing yourself in what you love:** Find that place where you're so immersed in what you're doing that you don't even notice yourself doing it. You surrender entirely to the moment. Everything feels effortless. For me, it feels like experiencing everything in slow motion. Painting, writing, dancing, playing music, running – whatever makes you forget the time, whatever pulls you so deeply into the moment that nothing else exists. It's not effort; it's ease.

The most important thing? It has to feel real to you – authentic. Something that makes your heart feel alive.

Presence isn't about doing something; it's about feeling something. It's about letting yourself be moved, be alive, and letting it resonate deep inside of you.

In a Nutshell

Presence is not a destination but a continuous unfolding. It's available in every breath, every **mo**vement – waiting for you to show up simply. A real gift. It doesn't last forever, but maybe that's what makes it so precious. Allow yourself the peace and grace of the moment. Show up for it. Feel it. And when you find yourself in those moments where life feels like enough, where you feel like enough, let it light you up. Let it remind you of what really matters.

Seize the moment, my dear friend! This is it. Here. Now. And it's beautiful. So, take a deep breath. Look around. Feel your heartbeat. A miracle

.

Reflective Questions

1. In which moments do you feel most present? And what does that moment feel like for you?
2. How does being fully present feel to you?
3. Which practices resonate most with you for cultivating presence? Why do you think they work for you?
4. How do you balance the paradox of living fully in the present while acknowledging its fleeting nature?
5. How can the compassionate component of presence – the wish for others to experience happiness – inform your daily interactions?
6. *You don't know the value of a moment until it becomes a memory.* What does this quote by Dr. Seuss mean to you?

Wake-up Prompts for being more present

1. Keep your whole heart wide open and let the inner flame of presence burn bright. Close your eyes and take three deep breaths. What do you notice about this exact moment right now?
2. Let your sense of perception open and scan your body now: What wants attention?
3. Can you describe a recent experience where you felt completely present and alive?
   a. What were you doing?
   b. How did it feel in your body, mind, and heart?
   c. What made it so special?
4. Remember an enthralling moment of your life. Try to describe or express it.
5. What keeps you from being present in your daily life?
   a. Are there specific distractions, habits, or thoughts that pull you away?
   b. How can you gently bring yourself back to the moment?
6. Write about an ordinary moment that felt extraordinary.
   a. How did presence transform it?

    b. Did it change the way you viewed your surroundings, yourself, or someone else?

7. Write a short story about someone experiencing true presence for the first time.
   a. What triggers this experience?
   b. How do they change as a result of it?
   c. Write a dialogue between two people where words are few, but presence says everything: How do their actions, silences, or body language convey their connection?

8. Imagine presence as a place.
   a. What does it look like?
   b. How do you feel when you're there?
   c. What happens to time in this space?

9. Compose a letter to yourself encouraging more presence in your life: What would you say to remind yourself to slow down and savor the moment?

10. Write a poem about the paradox of the present moment: Focus on its fleeting beauty, its quiet power, and how it connects us to life.

11. **Manifest**: *I have no time to rush! I go half pace, perceive twice as much, and in a different way. Pause. I sense the mystery and sacredness. I don't race across the surface. I go from trance to presence. I'm coming home to the present moment and feel the intimacy that surrounds me.*

GRATITUDE — The Practice of Appreciation

græ.tɪ.tjuːd

⠛⠗⠁⠑⠞⠊⠞⠥⠙

[Gratitude, thankfulness, or gratefulness stems from the Latin word *grātitūdō*, which means »pleasing,« »thankful,« or »agreeable,« and from old French *gratitude*, the quality of being thankful; readiness to show appreciation for and to return kindness]

Let us rise up and be thankful, for if we didn't learn a lot today, at least we learned a little,
and if we didn't learn a little, at least we didn't get sick,
and if we got sick, at least we didn't die;
so, let us all be thankful.
– *Buddha*

Gratitude (to be grateful, gratefully) – isn't it the key to a more meaningful life? Expressing gratitude expands our hearts, we feel better. Yet, in the busyness of our thoughts and goals, we often forget something as simple as saying **thank you** or showing appreciation.

There is this beautiful saying: *What we appreciate appreciates.* We first learn to value the service of others in our earliest years. We are born into 'thank you', and we die into 'thank you'. This is so profound. Sometimes, we don't realize the value of such profound moments. But I believe we can grasp the love behind the immensity.

What's more important than simply thinking about gratitude and realizing that we should be grateful, expressing it. While reflecting and praying with gratitude can be healing, expressing it makes it more tangible, for others and for us. It becomes a blessing, strengthening our relationships and fueling deeper connections.

Thankfulness is so woven into our culture that its importance is often overlooked. For instance, Thanksgiving is one of the most significant festive celebrations, particularly in the Anglo-American tradition.

Watering your Soul with Gratitude

There is so much goodness in life if only we choose to see it. Every day offers us the chance to be conscious of how deeply blessed we are, touched by the love and sacrifices of our parents and the beauty of existence itself. Gratitude wells up within us like a gentle stream, releasing love and peace to everything and everyone we feel moved to acknowledge. It draws us closer to the present moment – the eternal now – where life unfolds in its purest form.

Gratitude humbles us, reminding us of the vastness of life's gifts, while uplifting us with a sense of contentment and purpose. It weaves meaning into our past, grants peace for today, and inspires hope for tomorrow. It is a measure of our aliveness, a reflection of how attuned we are to the beauty around and within us.

Wherever we find ourselves in life, this is the perfect entry point for appreciation. Begin here, with self-appreciation. Water your own Spirit with kindness, speak gently to yourself, and nurture the roots of your Soul. Gratitude doesn't just transform the way we see life – it transforms the way we live it.

What makes us grateful?

We feel gratitude most intensely in moments of deep pain, grief, or suffering, whether for ourselves or for loved ones. These humbling experiences remind us of what we have and prompt us to give thanks. Challenging times teach us to seek and appreciate blessings more deeply.

But the most seemingly obvious things are often the most valuable. When we consciously think about our true gifts, the gifts we have been given, they awaken an instant appreciation. Blessings such as:
- Breathing
- Waking up
- Moving our body
- Eating a warm meal
- Sensing
- Hugging

- Learning and applying things
- Awe & wonder
- Thanksgiving

Simply pausing to ask, *what am I thankful for today?* can bring us into the present moment and work wonders for our mindset. For me, stark moments in nature make me pause and spark thankfulness, like when the sun rises over the Alpine ridge or goes to sleep and the golden hour sets in.

Often, it's the simplest and smallest things that mean the most. As A.A. Milne, author of Winnie-the-Pooh, wrote: *The smallest things take up the most room in your heart*. Small gestures can fill us with joy and gratitude. Learning to see the extraordinary in the ordinary –and to appreciate what we already have – is a powerful way to live a meaningful, blessed life.

The Bible has great wisdom, as in Luke 6:38: *Give, and it will be given to you*. Giving and serving others fosters gratitude. We came into this world with nothing, and we will leave with nothing. Sharing what we have with someone who needs it more brings immense satisfaction and meaning. Offering blessings and expressing gratitude ensures that others feel seen and appreciated.

What does Gratitude give us?

Focusing on what has been given to us, on what we already have, rather than yearning for more, cultivates a sense of thankfulness and happiness. In other words, to see giftedness in every aspect of life is one of the precious treasures. Gratitude shifts our attention to the positives in life and nurtures humility and contentment. It brings us to an inner silence – vast, still, and complete. Remember the words of David Steindl-Rast, *it is not happiness that makes us grateful, it is gratefulness that makes us happy*.

We shouldn't take anything for granted – even the ability to breathe. Breath is life, and through it, we connect with others. It's literally how we speak! Our very existence relies on countless interconnections, reminding us that life itself is a reason to be grateful.

When we appreciate life's blessings, even the smallest ones, we invite serenity into our hearts. Cultivating thankfulness is a simple yet **profound way to nurture inner peace**, as both are rooted in living mindfully and embracing the beauty of the moment. Together, they create harmony within and around us.

Even on cloudy days, we can find sunshine if we look for it. A thankful heart elevates our perspective, allowing us to focus on the good we already possess. That's why I always try to end each personal meeting with a hug and a »thank you« – you never know if you'll get another chance to see that person again. It's my way of honoring each encounter, knowing how precious these moments of connection really are.

So, be grateful. Be kind, not always right. Make others feel valued. **Thank YOU**, my dear friend, for taking the time to read these lines.

Thought Experiment

Imagine that you have achieved everything you wanted. All your goals and all your dreams are checked. Do you think you would have been humbled enough in such a scenario? Would there be enough room for gratitude?

Do not forget your humility. Modesty should find a daily place in your eagerness and ambition. So be careful for the love of more and me-first lifestyle. You risk losing appreciation of your God-given blessings.

A friendly Reminder – Celebrate Gratitude

Gratitude is the light we turn on that allows us to see, acknowledge, and maybe even embrace the invitation that the moment offers us. Take a moment each day to ask yourself, *what am I thankful for today?* Express your appreciation openly – say **thank you**, give to others, or show kindness in small ways. Always think how blessed you are. Recognize and focus on what you have, not what's missing, and find joy in life's simplest moments. In times of struggle, look for lessons and blessings to stay grounded. Try to cultivate thankfulness daily to build stronger relationships, nurture inner peace, and live a happier, appreciative, more fulfilled life.

> If the only prayer you ever say in your entire life is – Thank You – it will be enough.
> – *Meister Eckhart*

Reflective Questions

1. Today, have you said *thank you* to God, the universe, or what you believe in?
2. For what are you thankful?
3. Do you have a daily thankful practice?
4. What have been your most thankful moments in life so far?
5. Have you expressed gratitude to another person or blessed another person recently?
6. How does the tone of your voice change when expressing genuine gratitude versus a casual »thanks«?
7. What's the most meaningful thank you you've ever received? What made it so special?
8. When was the last time you wrote a handwritten note of thanks, and how did it feel?
9. What do *trading expectation for appreciation* and *having an attitude of gratitude* mean to you personally?
10. Sometimes, life hangs by a thread. We are lucky to (still) be alive. Have you ever had the feeling that you are extremely lucky to be alive?

Wake-up Prompts for Gratitude

1. Count your blessings of today.
2. Reflecting on your day: A moment that you really appreciated today was...
3. Write down what you are grateful for every day and week. »I'm thankful for...«. You can also say it every day for

what you are grateful for. I find this especially important because you never know how long you can say or write it to someone or something.

4. Thank someone for what she or he has given to you or for what they mean to you. Surprise this person with a note, gift, or sign of appreciation.

5. Prayer is one way to express gratitude. If you feel ready, say a thankful prayer to yourself or someone else.

6. Give thanks to someone who needs your help. Sometimes these are signs of what life has gifted you with.

7. What is one thing you have never before been thankful for? Try to be grateful for it.

8. »If I could thank my younger Self for one thing, it would be...«

9. »The hardest time I've had expressing gratitude was when...«

10. »Gratitude has transformed my relationship with... because...«

11. What's your earliest memory of feeling truly grateful?

12. When do you find it most challenging to express genuine gratitude?

13. *Be thankful for the small things; it is in them that your strength lies.* - Mother Teresa. What's one small act of kindness you witnessed today that deserves acknowledgment?

GIFTS — Recognizing and sharing your Blessings

gɪfts
∷ ⸫ ⸚ ⸴ ⸵

[**a:** that which is given, **b:** natural talent]

> What you are is God's gift to you,
> what you do with yourself is your gift to God.
> – *Danish Proverb*

Gifts (giftedness, to give, being gifted) are **blessings** from the Higher Power, our Source. The very fact that we are here, alive in this moment. The first gift is the one from the eternal world. As John O'Donohue beautifully put it: *Our very presence in the world is itself the first gift and primal blessing.* Or as Rainer Maria Rilke expresses so perfectly: *Hier zu sein ist so viel –* »simply being here is immense.« The magnitude of our Being is such a profound gift that we can hardly grasp it.

Think about the gifts you carry within you – your talents (aptitudes, inclinations, proclivity, abilities, you name it), your opportunities, your unique way of seeing the world. These do not come by coincidence; they were carefully woven into who you are by something greater than yourself. It's like they were chosen specifically for you, touching your heart in ways only you can fully understand.

And then there's the magic that happens when we share gifts with each other. Ever noticed how giving someone a heartfelt gift lights up not just their face, but yours too? It's like we're channeling that same generous Spirit that blessed us with our own gifts. Listening to our inner gifts, our Soul activity, and bringing them into the world is beautiful and enriching.

Gifts are treasures life offers. They grow from the eternal and are personal revelations to the recipient. Those who appreciate their gifts gain valuable insight into themselves and the world around them. **Gifts unfold when** they are not kept to oneself but **passed on**. True gifts can only be understood with the heart. In other words, the true power of a gift lies in sharing it with others, as it can only be truly understood with an open heart.

Gifts are very personal and should be cherished and received with gratitude, as they have the ability to strengthen relationships and touch the lives of people around the world. They strengthen relationships, true friendship, and have a very strong and deep effect on the recipient over the wider world.

Honestly, what is more beautiful than receiving a heart-touching gift from someone? A true gift comes without the intention of anything in return. A gift is given to give somebody a blessing, to make them richer in heart, to make them grateful.

When do we become aware of our Gifts?

More often than not, gifts live with us, but we do not really recognize them in a conscious manner. They are omni**present** but often do not unfold themselves in our daily lives and thus often go unnoticed.

Gifts become more present when we deeply think about things or when we have a crisis. During moments of reflection – often triggered by a personal crisis – we truly recognize and appreciate them. In those moments, we become aware of how lucky we are and how much life has to offer.

What about Forgiveness?

A gift is for the giver. This is accentuated by forgiveness. For**give**ness is the willingness to see beyond what has been done to us. When we forgive others, we are giving them a chance to start anew. It frees us from the burden of holding grudges and allows us to open ourselves up to new experiences and relationships. Without forgiveness, we may be stuck in the past and unable to move forward toward a happier future. So, let us practice forgiveness and giving to ourselves and others.

When do Gifts have their greatest Effect?

Do you know when gifts really shine? When they come straight from the heart, without any strings attached. It's never about the thing itself – it's about the thought, the intentionality, the love be- hind it that truly matters. That's the real gift behind the gift.

I hope these words find their way to your heart and maybe, just maybe, become a small, benevolent gift themselves. Because in sharing our thoughts about gifts, we're already participating in this beautiful cycle of giving and receiving that makes life so rich. Thank you, my dear friend, for reading this book!

In a Nutshell

Today is like any other day, and yet it holds immense power. Life has given you this amazing gift – simply being here. Just this awareness can change everything. You carry unique talents and opportunities within you, gifts meant specifically for you. Sometimes, you might not even notice these gifts in your daily life, but during quiet moments or challenging times – you real- ize just how blessed you are. When you share your gifts with others – whether through a thoughtful present, a kind gesture, or offering forgiveness – you create something beautiful. It's not about what you give but the heart behind it. Your gifts be- come most powerful when you share them openly, touching others' lives and strengthening your connections. So, uncover the gold within you. Remember, you are a gift to this world, and your presence matters. Are you ready to give yourself away?

Reflective Questions

1. Remember, whatever you are gifted in is the key to your prosperity: What gifts do you offer to the world? What is a gift you gave someone last time?
2. Do you think you have unique talents? What are these special talents?

3. Are you thankful for gifts, and in which way? When was the last time you felt deeply grateful for a gift in your life?
4. What unique gifts do you carry that you might not have fully recognized yet?
5. How has a challenge or crisis helped you discover hidden gifts within yourself?
6. Do you think what you give wholeheartedly will be given to you?
7. What do you think you haven't given yet?
8. Do you think everything and everybody is a gift?
9. What gift have you been withholding from the world? Why?

Wake-up Prompts for Gifts

1. Surprise someone with a gift of appreciation.
2. *A friend is a gift you give yourself.* What does this quote by Robert Louis Stevenson mean to you?
3. Write about a moment when someone's gift touched your heart deeply. What made it so special?
4. Describe three gifts you've received from life that money can't buy.
5. How could you share your unique gifts with others in a meaningful way?
6. Daily practices:
   a. Each morning, acknowledge one gift in your life you might usually take for granted.
   b. Before going to sleep, reflect on one way you shared your gifts with others today.
   c. Practice seeing challenges as opportunities to discover new gifts within yourself.

MOTIVATION — Sustaining your Journey

ˌmoʊ.tɪˈveɪ.ʃən

⠍⠕⠲⠞⠊⠧⠑⠊⠲⠱⠩⠝

[a reason or reasons for acting or behaving in a particular way; from the Latin term *motivus* – »a moving cause«]

> If your why isn't big enough, your excuses will be.
> – *Unknown Author*

U nderstanding the true essence of Motivation (to motivate, motivated) – its purpose, effects, and underlying mechanisms – is vital for applying it effectively in life. Despite the vast array of literature on the subject, the core idea often remains elusive.

Motivation contains the word **motive**, which implies a **reason** or purpose for taking action. At its core, motivation seeks to answer the question of **why** something is done, exploring the origin or driving forces behind a behavior. Its focus is less on the action itself but more on the impetus or stimulus, the moving cause, or the spark that initiates and sustains the behavior.

Why the Term »Motivation« is often misunderstood

When we come across the word »motivation«, we often associate it with overcoming challenges or achieving something special. It gives us a feeling of excitement or drive, leading us to think in terms of goals and rewards – the outcomes or »what« – rather than considering the deeper meaning behind the actions – the true reasons **why** we do something effectively.

Often, we know what we want or need to do and what motivates us. However, we are struggling to find the immediate energy to do the task right now, leading to procrastination. Or we do it, but not for a very long time, as we become disturbed, injected with someone else's goals. These are typically pull motives, which represent extrinsic or externally imposed goals or actions for which one is not enormously enthusiastic. Such motives can feel less personal, often centering on achieving a specific outcome rather than being fueled by intrinsic passion.

In contrast, intrinsic motivation arises from within. It is tied to actions that provide inherent satisfaction or joy. Unlike extrinsic motivation, which is driven by external rewards like recognition or monetary gain, intrinsic motivation focuses on the pleasure and fulfillment derived directly from the action itself. In that sense, intrinsic motivation can be seen as the true means to an end.

Ideally, intrinsic and extrinsic motivations work in tandem. While intrinsic motivation aligns you more with your true calling, extrinsic incentives can act as supportive tools for achieving specific tasks. Regardless of the approach you follow, the essence of motivation lies in understanding **why** you are doing something.

Why knowing your »WHY« is essential

Motivation is not a constant; it goes up and down like a sensation that lights up our emotions before they extinguish. We all have this moody experience. But why is it then important to know one's motive? Because it gives clarity as to **why** one starts each day energized or accomplishes one's activities with energy and joy. When you are clear about your motives, you can align your future activities accordingly and better articulate your goals in conversations, which also helps and, in the best case, inspires fellow human Beings.

Of course, there is always a **why** behind the way; it's an endless cycle. The key is to connect with your heart-driven feeling, that supportive inner voice that abides and guides you throughout your life. As long as you stay connected to this deep inner voice and align your actions with it, you are on the right track.

How to nurture and increase Motivation

Incentives trigger your emotions, and emotions are the juice for doing something. Therefore, setting the right incentives is key. Here are some helpful ideas that invite you to take action:

- **Create an optimal Environment:** Design your workspace or surroundings to support your goals and minimize distractions.
- **Plan and prioritize:** Schedule your activities and allow time for tasks you are genuinely passionate about.
- **Use visual Reminders:** Stickers, memos, or notes can help you refocus your attention on preferred activities.
- **Incorporate positive Messaging:** Daily affirmations or motivational notifications can provide consistent encouragement.
- **Set achievable Goals:** Breaking tasks into manageable weekly goals fosters a sense of accomplishment.

While understanding your why is essential, motivation often follows action rather than preceding it. For example, think about the satisfying feeling you get during or after your workout, not before it. Action creates momentum, which can further fuel motivation, forming a virtuous cycle of energy and productivity.

Understanding your Motives

But how do we understand our motives? One effective approach is to use an impact model:

1. **Curiosity**: Our innate drive to explore and learn sparks initial interest.
2. **Interest**: This curiosity evolves into focused attention on certain activities or topics.
3. **Passion**: Sustained interest transforms into a deeper commitment.
4. **Purpose**: Over time, passion crystallizes into a clear, guiding objective.

While curiosity fuels exploration, motivation manifests in deliberate action, driven by specific interests and passions. It shows itself in what we like to do, in our interests and heightened interests or passions, which then consciously or unconsciously develop into a purpose over the course of time. In fact, time will tell our true motives – we cannot hide our real identity from others and ourselves.

Motivation, Goals, and Purpose in Harmony

Motivation, goal, vision, and purpose are congruent in the best case. Each of these terms is preceded by the question of **WHY**. Ideally, the main triggering moment comes from within, with supportive mechanisms from outside. What seems essential is that it gives you a good feeling and energy.

In an ideal scenario, motivation, goals, vision, and purpose align seamlessly. Each of these elements revolves around the question of **why**. When the driving force comes primarily from within, supported by external mechanisms, it provides you with sustained energy and fulfillment. Ultimately, the key to mastering motivation lies in understanding your »why« and leveraging it to take meaningful action, even when your drive falters.

Motivation is...

Drive – incentive – the quest for the why – the why behind the action – the why behind the why – the WHY itself – the reason – the higher reason – the spark – the trigger – the impetus – the reason – searching for the heart-driven inner voice – feel your why – stimulus – impulse – catalyst – desire – ambition – determination – willpower – enthusiasm (originally Greek meaning *inspired by God within*) – dedication – aspiration – energy – zest – initiative – urge – provocation – encouragement – stimulation – push – a feeling of anticipation, determination, eagerness, and excitement

In a Nutshell

Motivation drives our actions, fueled by reasons that inspire us. It sparks excitement and determination, but can also bring pressure or frustration. Knowing your **why** helps you stay focused, energized, and aligned with your goals.

Reflective Questions

1. What motivates you most in life, and why?
2. Are you actively searching for your why?
3. When do you feel the most energized and driven? What triggers motivation for you?
4. Do you know your "WHYs"? Think about them – How do you feel?
5. Are you more intrinsically or extrinsically motivated? Try to find intrinsically motivated actions.
6. Has your motivation changed over the years?
7. *Opportunities don't happen. You create them.* What do you think about this quote from Chris Grosser? Do you create your opportunities?
8. What small action could you take today to boost your motivation?

Wake-up Prompts for Motivation

1. Write down the activities you are particularly interested in or passionate about and try to give them the space and place they need in your life.
2. Describe a moment when you felt incredibly motivated. What sparked it?
3. Write about your biggest "why" – the reason that drives you to act.
4. Take daily actions on these activities so that they become a habit and hence are done automatically.
5. Think of a positive phrase or sentence that reverberates with your deep inner guiding voice and say it to yourself several times today.
6. Visualize your ideal future. How does motivation play a role in achieving it?
7. Write down a motivational quote that resonates with you and why it inspires you.
8. Create a list of rewards you could use to celebrate small wins.

DEATH — Embracing Life's ultimate Teacher

dεθ

∷ ∵ ⸳ ⸴∷

[the process, act, condition of dying]

> The best way to prepare for death
> is to live life to its fullest.
> – *John Bytheway*

D eath (to die, dying) is the release of life itself, the moment of ultimate surrender. Death is always with us. It walks with us, whether we choose to notice it or not – **our silent, constant companion**. Every day, something within us dies – an idea, a belief, a version of ourselves. Even without the physical death of the body, we are perpetually shedding and evolving. Indeed, small deaths, I call them life renewals or restorations, are necessary to make room for something new.

Death is our fate; it's always here with us. When we listen carefully, we sense death as the **place of total presence**. Paradoxically, it is this awareness of death that opens our eyes to the beauty of life. Knowing our time is finite makes every moment precious. The ego may not want to hear about death. But it would heal it. What if we were given an unlimited amount of time – would we still cherish the present? Would we still feel the urgency to create, to love, to grow? Perhaps not. The significance of a single day might fade into the monotony of eternity.

The Map of Death

Death is the ultimate equalizer – the democracy of the grave. We cannot un-deadify our life (only the unlived one). There is no way out, just through, for all of us. I think we are aware that we are going to die someday, and I'm speaking of death at the end of our earthly lifetime. With our last breath, life goes out of us. Any tension that is still present is released with this last breath. Even if death is so omnipresent, we still don't want to look death in the eye, or at least want to delay it. Personally, I am not afraid of death itself, but rather of losing consciousness. I imagine my father shining like a star in the sky, holding onto the hope – no, I know it in my heart of hearts – that we remain connected beyond his, beyond our earthly death. When death knocks, it is not just an ending but, at the same time, a new beginning. It's a **transformation** (as everything in life is at any given moment); during dying, as with creation, we simply **transition into another form**, another structure, an altered state. I see death as a rebirth into a new life form – a journey from immanence to transcendence. It's a metamorphosis, a transfiguration that awaits all of us. Or, as Ram Dass beautifully put it: *We are all just walking each other home.*

Death opens our Eyes and teaches us Humility

Death is maybe the **ultimate teacher** that compels us to live each moment mindfully and meaningfully. When we are young, we feel immortal. However, our passing reminds us of the fragility of existence. In its shadow, life appears delicate and fleeting. This awareness invites humility – an acknowledgment of the vast, uncontrollable forces that shape our lives. To stand before the inevitability of death is to understand how small we truly are and yet how meaningful each fleeting moment can be.

When death arrives, when our bodies, all our emotions, die, I believe it will become the ultimate aha-moment. It will be the opening of the portal to eternal light. Because dying is a process – the brain and the cells are still alive when our heart stops pumping, and we breathe out for the last time. I had a personal experience in my early twenties when I lost consciousness, and when I came back to consciousness, my life was revealed to me like a film.

Death is the Companion and Friend of a Life worth living

If we embrace death not as an enemy but as a companion, it can become a teacher. It nudges us toward presence, urging us to focus on what truly matters. It strips away the noise and brings clarity to our priorities. When you look death in the eye, it will reflect life. The secret –you – sees itself – yourself.

Perhaps the greatest gift death offers is the perspective to reverse-engineer our lives. By imagining the end – our final moments, the legacy we leave behind – we can design a life worth living. An examined and luminous life. Start at the finish line: What kind of person do you want to be remembered as? What impact do you want to have? From there, craft your life not as a rigid plan but as a guiding framework, a compass pointing toward your deepest values.

Life and Death are One

Life and death are inseparable companions. Without one, the other cannot exist. They **are a loving couple**. Death is really a day of birth. It gives life its meaning, its urgency, its beauty.

Even at the very beginning of our journey – our birth – we experience both life and death. To enter the visible world, we must leave behind the oneness of our mother's womb. When the cut is made, we take our first inbreath. It is both a beginning and an ending, the αlpha and the Ωmega, a tiny death that makes life possible.

The fragile Gift of Time

My Friend, you are going to die; I'm going to die. We both, we all, have an expiration date. We have just so many precious moments. Our time here is finite, measured not in the endless expanse of eternity but in the fragile, fleeting moments of a single lifetime. And that is what makes life so extraordinary. Death is not here to take life from us but to remind us to live fully, boldly, and with gratitude. Thus, sensing and cherishing the space of presence, the spaciousness, gives us so much.

Letting go is inevitable, but it can be brutally hard. Heartbreaks and regrets of missed opportunities will haunt us. We try to escape them. But there is no escape, just acceptance. In these difficult moments of our lives, it helps to reflect on gratitude. It makes the day seem a little brighter and more comforting.

The confrontation with **death brings humility and grace**. When we walk hand in hand with death, it doesn't have to be a shadow over our lives. Instead, it can be a light, illuminating what matters most. Indeed, a meaningful path involves little deaths for a greater, larger life to emerge. Or in the words of the Benedictine monk David Steindl-Rast: *Our inner world must become overwhelmed and almost destroyed; only then can the life-saving, world-renewing energies be found.*

Thought Experiment – Are we willing to die early for what truly matters to us?

In other words, how much would you give up for what you care about? This profound question reaches its peak when we consider sacrificing our lives for our deepest beliefs.

History shows many who chose principles over survival, from Socrates to modern activists. But this deeply personal question asks us to examine our core values against the ultimate price.

Consider what you cherish most: family, beliefs, life's work, or moral principles. When faced with mortality, our true priorities emerge clearly. The question challenges us to define a meaningful life – is longevity more valuable than authenticity?

Paradoxically, **the things we might die for** – love, aliveness, meaningful pursuits – **make life worth living**. Our willingness to sacrifice for them affirms their fundamental importance. In exploring what we would die for, we discover what we need to live for.

In a Nutshell – Life through the Lens of Death

Death is not an enemy but a friendly companion that reminds you to live with intention. By embracing its presence, you gain clarity on what truly matters. Reverse-engineering life – starting at the end and envisioning how we want to be remembered – helps us design a life filled with purpose and meaning.

Death inspires you to focus on your values, strip away distractions, and live boldly. It's the gentle nudge that keeps you present and reminds you of the fragile gift of time. When you walk along-side death, it opens your eyes to the beauty of life and the significance of every moment. Therefore, my friend, remember Les Brown's advice: *Live your life the way you want to leave your life.*

Remember, any day can be your last day. Give yourself the permission to be who you really are, finally, before you are no longer here – breathe life to the full!

Reflective Questions

1. What is life without death for you? What is the significance of death?
2. Do you have a life plan?
3. Do you think our meaning and purpose become clear(er) from the perspective of our own mortality?
4. If you died now, would you have any regrets?
5. How will you feel if conscious on your deathbed that you had not been here as yourself?
6. Imagine your last day. What do you want to look back on and feel proud of?
7. Write your own eulogy. What values, actions, and relationships would you want it to highlight?
8. If someone were to summarize your life in one sentence, what would you want it to say?
9. How would your priorities change if you only had a year left to live?
10. What has your awareness of mortality taught you about life?
11. How does reflecting on death affect your gratitude for what you have?
12. Would you feel more pressure if you had only one year to live from now? Shouldn't you focus more on the sacred pause and not rush any longer through life?

Wake-up Prompts

1. *Death is not the greatest loss in life. The greatest loss is what dies inside us while we live.* – Norman Cousins. What does this quote mean to you? What would you like to re-awaken that you have forgotten with time?
2. Imagine you are at the end of your physical earthly life. What would you want to say about yourself and your life?
3. Write about a time when loss helped you see life in a new light.
4. The closer you get to your statistically "expected" death on Earth, the more you probably think about your own mortality. Try to embrace death a little bit more. See how grateful you become if you do this. It opens a whole new world for you if you see life in perspective.
5. If death didn't exist, what would change about how humans approach life? Would it make life less meaningful?
6. Write a letter to your future Self from the perspective of the end of your life.
7. Describe a conversation between yourself and "Death" as a person. What would death tell you about your life?
8. Explore the idea: "Life and death are not opposites but partners." How does this perspective change your understanding of both?
9. What does the following quote attributed to Confucius mean to you: *Every man has two lives, and the second one begins when you realize you have just one.*

Reflect on the **top five regrets of the dying** by Bronnie Ware:
- **Regret I**: I wish I'd had the courage to live a life true to myself.
- **Regret II**: I wish I didn't work so hard.
- **Regret III**: I wish I'd had the courage to express my feelings.
- **Regret IV**: I wish I'd stayed in touch with my friends.
- **Regret V**: I wish I had let myself be happier.

Final Thoughts – the new Self

Reflecting on life's big questions has expanded my perspective. Some have lingered in my mind for days, revealing eye-opening moments over months, years in fact.

Self-discovery is an ongoing journey. It's a vocation to the inner world, an inside job of seeking oneself – »**me-search**.« This manuscript is a collection of personal experiences, a self-therapeutic anthology.

The answers to life's burning questions lie within the foundations of your Being. You are here, we are here to participate in our own unfolding, to awaken the secret lives that dwell within our Souls.

Personal Lessons learned from writing this Book:

- **Write spontaneously** – If a question resonates deeply, revisit and refine your response.
- **The more you write, the more connections you uncover** – Habitual writing clarifies insights and strengthens the art of writing a book.
- **Questions fuel discovery** – Answers lead to more questions, creating a self-reinforcing cycle.
- **Taking a pause helps** – Sometimes it no longer felt clear to me. The chapters numbed me, I didn't understand anything anymore, any longer. Grinding work. I no longer saw meaning in writing this meaningful book. I needed a break.
- **Me-search** – We are in search of ourselves. The one who teaches (writes) is the one who needs to be healed.

Change is a Process, not an Event

Lasting transformation is not a single moment but an ongoing evolution. Our time here on this spinning planet we call Earth is precious – meant for creation and adventure, not distractions.

To facilitate meaningful change:

1. **Clarify your Lessons:** Identify key insights and focus on deliberate growth.
2. **Reflect regularly:** Integration takes time; patience is essential.
3. **See with your Heart:** Let your heart speak.

Socrates wisely noted: *The secret of change is to focus all of your energy not on fighting the old, but on building the new.* Never fight little fires. **Keep your eye on the bigger vision.**

Living fully

What brings you to life? What experiences offer the most profound lessons? Never doubt that **your story matters**. It does, and it is a **gift to the world**! Each of your journeys contributes to the tapestry of human experience in ways you may never fully comprehend. And that's completely OK!

What new horizon within you is waiting to be seen? What aspects of your potential remain unexpressed? There is no single path but infinite, unique ways to live an integrated life. Trust what resonates and pursue it wholeheartedly.

And yes, life flows between ease and challenge. Some days feel light and effortless; others are heavy and slow – time feels like it's on standby. A balanced variability helps – knowing when to persist and when to adapt.

As we grow older, or better, grow into age (this is beautifully captured in the English language), we gain perspective. Death dances with us, celebrating life alongside us. This awareness enriches our experience rather than diminishes it. Show your aliveness. Put your heart and Soul into something meaningful. At the end of our earthly life, we become more interested in the profound, full moments we've experienced. Time is precious – use it for what truly moves you. Even from our humble not-knowing, we can offer something to others. Express gratitude for simply being alive – the magnitude of being.

Creating an integrated Life

True fulfillment isn't about perfection – it's about wholeness, embracing our strengths and weaknesses, joys and sorrows, knowing and not-knowing. Living life with all its unbearable beauty, the galaxy of bliss, and unfathomable pain, the ocean of tears.

The moments we create and cherish become the quintessence, the pearls, of an integrated life. The treasures of our existence. Through this integration, we discover what it truly means to live a fulfilled life – one moment, one choice, one breath at a time.

Every moment holds infinite possibilities. What if one defining moment is ahead, ready to change everything? Growth comes from challenging ourselves, stepping beyond comfort. Believe me, there is so much more to discover beyond the confines of our comfortable routines.

An Invitation to Self-Reflection

Now I invite you to ask yourself: **What is the best life you can imagine?** What is the most extraordinary version of yourself, your dream life, so to speak, you envision? Let these reflections accompany and guide you. Struggles will arise, but they will dignify and ennoble your Soul and enrich your journey, inspiring others in turn.

Above all, I really hope you have reverence for your life. Cultivate gratitude, enthusiasm, and a sense of wonder. Celebrate the remarkable gift of existence in all its forms.

The Path to Self-Discovery

John O'Donohue's wise words remind us: *The dream of every life is to realize itself.* We will be confronted with what we suppress. The more you suppress and resist your calling, the stronger it will manifest itself – the return of the repressed. You cannot neglect your calling – life's summons. I encourage you not to hold back. Especially not resting on »an easy life,« not relying on it, it will never be easy at all. Do not deny yourself adventure, but experience the life that's waiting for you beneath the surface of comfort and routine. Your unlived life will show up along the way, and that's fine. I find that people often try to rationalize away, really avoid, the magnitude of their unlived lives, their shadow.

Don't deny your shadow. Follow your heroic journey anyway, anyhow. **Try, at least, try. Trust life**. The path may not be apparent, but your heart already knows the way if you're willing to listen.

Don't get sidetracked. Don't live a small, diminished life but a life that outlives you.

What brings you true fulfillment? A sense of enrichment? What speaks to your Soul, engages your Spirit? Creating something you are proud to share is a sign you are working at your highest level.

Seizing Life's Possibilities

Every moment is filled with endless possibilities. What if you knew that there is a divine moment coming in such a way that nothing will be the same again? One defining moment that determines the course of your life.

Every moment seeks expression through you. Mortality ensures we make the most of it.

Sometimes, all it takes is:

- Living your questions
- A slight shift in perspective – for example, from *will it work?* to *is it worth trying?*
- Seeing abundance over scarcity, opportunities over problems
- Avoiding the hedonic treadmill
- Finding goodness in every action
- Living a life with dignity and grace

It is my hope that this book will serve as a resource for you, for each of us to reconnect with the deep respect for what resides within us. Your dreams know, your blood knows, your bones know what you wish, what you desire, what you know. You are often closer than you think, my dear friend. You deserve this journey. May you be brave enough to **realize your dream – and,** in doing so, **change everything for us all.**

Bibliography

Barks, C. (Ed.). (2004). *The essential Rumi* (New expanded ed.). HarperOne.

Brach, T. (Host). (2023, März 15). *Facing Fear (Part 1) – Awakening Your Fearless Heart* [Audio podcast episode]. In *Tara Brach*. Tara Brach. https://www.tarabrach.com/facing-fear-part-1-awakening-your-fearless-heart/

Brach, T. (2019). *Radical compassion: Learning to love yourself and your world with the practice of RAIN*. Viking.

Brown, B. (2017). *Braving the wilderness: The quest for true belonging and the courage to stand alone*. Random House.

Brown, L. (1992). *Live your dreams*. HarperCollins.

Campbell, J. (1991). *Reflections on the art of living: A Joseph Campbell companion* (D. K. Osbon, Ed.). HarperCollins.

Clavien, C. (2009). Review of *Gut Feelings: Short Cuts to Better Decision Making* by G. Gigerenzer. *Ethics, Theory and Moral Practice, 13*(2), 113–115. https://doi.org/10.1007/s10677-009-9172-8

Cohen, M. J. (1997). *Reconnecting with Nature: Finding Wellness through Restoring Your Bond with the Earth*. Ecopress.

Diener, E., & Seligman, M. E. P. (2002). Very happy people. *Psychological Science, 13*(1), 81–84. https://doi.org/10.1111/1467-9280.00415

Dyer, W. (2004). *The power of intention: Learning to co-create your world your way*. Hay House.

Frankl, V. E. (2006). *Man's search for meaning: An introduction to logotherapy* (4th ed.). Beacon Press.

Hollis, J. (2009). *Through the dark wood: Finding meaning in the second half of life*. Sounds True.

Holt-Lunstad, J., Smith, T. B., & Layton, J. B. (2010). Social relationships and mortality risk: A meta-analytic review. *PLoS Medicine, 7*(7), e1000316. https://doi.org/10.1371/journal.pmed.1000316

Jung, C. G. (1964). *Man and his symbols* (C. G. Jung, Ed.). Doubleday.

Kabat-Zinn, J. (2005). *Wherever you go, there you are: Mindfulness meditation in everyday life*. Hachette Books.

Kaufman, S. B. (2020). *Transcend: The new science of self-actualization*. TarcherPerigee.

Keller, H. (1903). *The story of my life*. Dover Publications.

Maxwell, J. C. (2013). *The 15 invaluable laws of growth: Live them and reach your potential*. Thomas Nelson.

Milne, A. A. (1926). *Winnie-the-Pooh*. E. P. Dutton & Co.

Murchie, G. (n.d.). *Natural senses*. Greensong. Retrieved April 13, 2025, from https://www.greensong.info/natural-senses

Nepo, M. (2000). *The book of awakening: Having the life you want by being present to the life you have*. Conari Press.

O'Donohue, J. (1997). *Anam cara: A book of Celtic wisdom*. HarperCollins.

O'Donohue, J. (2003). *Beauty: The invisible embrace*. HarperCollins.

Oliver, M. (2016). *Upstream: Selected essays*. Penguin Press.

Pressfield, S. (2022). *Put your ass where your heart wants to be*. Black Irish Entertainment LLC.

Price-Mitchell, M. (n.d.). *Curiosity: How parents foster lifelong learning in children*. Roots of Action. Retrieved April 13, 2025, from https://www.rootsofaction.com/curiosity-lifelong-learning/

Ram Dass. (1971). *Be here now*. Consciousness Books.

Rilke, R. M. (1989). *The selected poetry of Rainer Maria Rilke* (S. Mitchell, Trans.). Vintage International. (Original work published 1923)

Rilke, R. M. (2004). *Letters to a young poet* (M. D. Herter Norton, Trans.). W.W. Norton & Company. (Original work published 1929)

Robbins, T. (1991). *Awaken the giant within: How to take immediate control of your mental, emotional, physical and financial destiny!* Summit Books.

Seligman, M. E. P., Railton, P., Baumeister, R. F., & Sripada, C. (2016). *Homo prospectus*. Oxford University Press.

Shakespeare, W. (1609). *Hamlet*. As cited in AZQuotes. Retrieved from https://www.azquotes.com/quote/518386

Siegel, D. J. (2016). *Mind: A journey to the heart of being human*. W.W. Norton & Company.

Smith, J. (2022). *Why has nobody told me this before?* HarperOne.

Steindl-Rast, D. (1991). *Gratefulness, the heart of prayer: An approach to life in full awareness*. Paulist Press.

St. Teresa of Avila. (2016). *The interior castle: A new translation* (M. Starr, Trans.). Shambhala. (Original work published 1588)

Thrash, T. M., & Elliot, A. J. (2003). Inspiration as a psychological construct. *Journal of Personality and Social Psychology, 84*(4), 871–889. https://psycnet.apa.org/doiLanding?doi=10.1037%2F0022-3514.84.4.871

The Holy Bible, New International Version. (2011). Zondervan.

Thoreau, H. D. (1987). *Walden and other writings* (B. Blaisdell, Ed.). Bantam Books. (Original works published in the 19th century)

Tolle, E. (2004). *The Power of Now: A Guide to Spiritual Enlightenment*. New World Library.

Waldinger, R. (2015). *What makes a good life? Lessons from the longest study on happiness* [TED Talk]. https://www.ted.com/talks/robert_waldinger_what_makes_a_good_life_lessons_from_the_longest_study_on_happiness

Ware, B. (2012). *The top five regrets of the dying: A life transformed by the dearly departing*. Hay House.

Whitman, W. (1892). *Leaves of grass*. Philadelphia: David McKay.

Wiest, B. (2016). *101 essays that will change the way you think*. Thought Catalog.

Yeats, W. B. (n.d.). *The world is full of magical things, patiently waiting for our senses to sharpen* [Quote]. Retrieved from https://www.goodreads.com/quotes/

Acknowledgments ·

I wish to thank

Manuela, for your specific questions and encouragement

Lilie, our sunshine, you inspire me every day

My Parents, for your dedication and wisdom

Friends who have supported and encouraged me in writing and publishing

My Ancestors, I wouldn't be here without you

God and the whole Universe for everything we need to live and all the blessings we receive.

THANK YOU